The Politics of Data Transfer

In this book, Yuko Suda examines the Safe Harbor debate, the passenger name record (PNR) dispute, and the Society for Worldwide Interbank Financial Transactions (SWIFT) affair to understand the transfer of personal data from the European Union (EU) to the United States. She argues that the Safe Harbor, PNR, and SWIFT agreements were made to mitigate the potentially negative effects that may arise from the beyond-the-border reach of EU data protection rules or US counterterrorism regulation. A close examination of these high-profile cases would reveal how beyond-the-border reach of one jurisdiction's regulation might affect another jurisdiction's policy and what responses the affected jurisdiction possibly makes to manage the effects of such extraterritorial regulation.

The Politics of Data Transfer adds another dimension to the study of transatlantic data conflicts by assuming that the cases exemplify not only the politics of data privacy but also the politics of extraterritorial regulation. A welcome and timely collection uncovering the evolution of and prospects for the politics of data privacy in the digitalized and interconnected world.

Yuko Suda is a part-time lecturer at Tokyo University of Foreign Studies, Japan.

Routledge Studies in Global Information, Politics and Society

Edited by Kenneth Rogerson, Duke University and Laura Roselle, Elon University

International communication encompasses everything from one-to-one cross-cultural interactions to the global reach of a broad range of information and communications technologies and processes. *Routledge Studies in Global Information*, Politics and Society celebrates – and embraces – this depth and breadth. To completely understand communication, it must be studied in concert with many factors, since, most often, it is the foundational principle on which other subjects rest. This series provides a publishing space for scholarship in the expansive, yet intersecting, categories of communication and information processes and other disciplines.

10. Beyond the Internet
Unplugging the Protest Movement Wave
Edited by Rita Figueiras and Paula do Espírito Santo

11. Twitter and Elections Around the World
Campaigning in 140 Characters or Less
Edited by Richard Davis, Christina Holtz-Bacha, and Marion Just

12. Political Communication in Real Time
Theoretical and Applied Research Approaches
Edited by Dan Schill, Rita Kirk, Amy Jasperson

13. Disability Rights Advocacy Online
Voice, Empowerment and Global Connectivity
Filippo Trevisan

14. Media Relations of the Anti-War Movement
The Battle for Hearts and Minds
Ian Taylor

15. The Politics of Data Transfer
Transatlantic Conflict and Cooperation over Data Privacy
Yuko Suda

16. The Media and the Public Sphere
A Deliberative Model of Democracy
Thomas Häussler

The Politics of Data Transfer

Transatlantic Conflict and Cooperation over Data Privacy

Yuko Suda

Routledge
Taylor & Francis Group
NEW YORK AND LONDON

First published 2018
by Routledge
605 Third Avenue, New York, NY 10017

and by Routledge
2 Park Square, Milton Park, Abingdon, Oxon OX14 4RN

Routledge is an imprint of the Taylor & Francis Group, an informa business

Library of Congress Cataloging-in-Publication Data
A catalog record for this book has been requested

ISBN: 978-1-138-69628-0 (hbk)
ISBN: 978-1-315-52485-6 (ebk)

Typeset in Bembo
by Taylor & Francis Books

Contents

Foreword vi
Acknowledgements vii

Introduction 1

1 The Politics of Data Privacy 10

2 The Politics of Extraterritorial Regulation 19

3 The EU Data Protection Directive 30

4 From Safe Harbor to Privacy Shield 38

5 The PNR Dispute 55

6 The EU PNR Directive 71

7 The SWIFT Affair 81

8 Data Privacy and Free Trade Agreements 94

9 Conclusion 109

References 121
Index 136

Foreword

By Kenneth Rogerson and Laura Roselle, series editors

In the early, heady days of internet diffusion, the term "borderless" was used to evoke the excitement of global communication in which traditional geopolitical boundaries were immaterial. Experience has taught us that this euphoria was never as real as it seemed. Yuko Suda dives deeply into the politics of global data flows, reminding us of how relevant the understanding of attempts to regulate these flows really are. While, at times, regulations feel piecemeal and even haphazard, their existence has consequences, both within countries and elsewhere. Understanding the relationship between global communication and the state has never been more important.

Acknowledgements

This book has evolved from my article, "Transatlantic Politics of Data Transfer: Extraterritoriality, Counter-Extraterritoriality and Counter-Terrorism," which was published in the *Journal of Common Market Studies* (*JCMS*), Volume 51, Issue 4, July 2013. The article is a comparative case study of the passenger name record (PNR) dispute, the Society of Worldwide Interbank Financial Transactions (SWIFT) affair, and the Container Security Initiative (CSI), focusing on the extraterritorial reach of the counterterrorism regulation of the United States (US) and the data protection regulation of the European Union (EU). My approach to analyzing these cases using the concept of extraterritoriality was influenced by an article by Miles Kahler and David A. Lake titled "Economic Integration and Global Governance: Why So Little Supranationalism?" (Walter Mattli and Ngaire Woods, eds, *The Politics of Global Regulation*, Princeton: Princeton University Press, 2009). In this sense, this book, which is an extension of my *JCMS* article, was inspired by the account of the SWIFT case that Kahler and Lake provided in their highly stimulating article.

A book cannot be produced with a wave of a magic wand. While it was a long and complicated process, I was fortunate to have received a lot of support and assistance. I greatly appreciate the helpful comments from the series editors, Kenneth Rogerson and Laura Roselle, as well as the two anonymous reviewers.

I am heartily thankful to David Wessels for his help, guidance, and encouragement during the writing of this book. I also would like to thank Yuichi Morii, who was kind enough to read my manuscript and offer valuable comments and suggestions with his expertise in EU politics.

I would like to express my gratitude to Kazuto Suzuki, Yoko Kawamura, and Fumio Shimpo for their kind assistance.

Part of the research for this book was presented at the 2011 Annual Convention of the Japan Association of International Relations. I am grateful to Yukio Maeda, Naofumi Miyasaka, Heigo Sato, and other participants in the session for their feedback.

The research for this book was furthered by a grant from the Telecommunications Advancement Foundation. With this financial support, I was able to fly to Brussels and conduct interviews with officials of the European Commission and with the European Data Protection supervisor, who kindly spared some time for me. I have also benefited from a research grant from the KDDI Foundation.

The manuscript of this book was edited for language by Editage. I never thought I would write a book in English, which is not my native language. But somehow I did.

Introduction

With advanced information communication technology, it is now routine to collect, process, use, store, and transfer various kinds of data across national borders. Cross-border flows of data, indeed, are soaring and connecting more countries, organizations, and people. According to one analysis, cross-border data flows grew 45 times larger between 2005 and 2014 (McKinsey Global Institute 2016). The rise of the internet, of course, has contributed to this exponential growth; between 2000 and 2015, internet penetration has increased almost sevenfold from 6.5 to 43 percent of the global population (ITU 2015). Recent technological developments, most notably "cloud computing," are further increasing the volume and complexity of data flows. Nowadays, data might be collected in Berlin, processed in Bangalore, stored in Boston, and accessed from Brisbane.

Among the enormous digital streams are data that contain personal information, such as names, addresses, telephone numbers, and email addresses. In fact, myriad activities undertaken by individuals and businesses—ranging from shopping at a "foreign" website to chatting with a friend abroad through a social networking service (SNS) to transnational corporations managing employee and customer records—generate flows of personal data across borders. In addition, some government activities also entail cross-border flows of personally identifiable information. Sharing of information between law enforcement authorities of different countries is a good example. By all accounts, cross-border flows of personal data are crucially important in economic, social, and political terms.

Significantly, while data flow across national borders and territoriality appears to be losing its salience in this field, collection, processing, use, storage, and transfer of personal data are regulated primarily by national data protection or privacy laws that are enacted and enforced within territorially based jurisdictions (Gellman 1999; Reidenberg 1999). This means that the reach of law or regulation is incongruent with the geographical scope of what is being regulated, possibly leading to overlapping jurisdictional claims by different states.

To make matters more complicated, there exist considerable differences among national data privacy laws and regulations, which in turn reflect differences in historical experiences, cultural values, and beliefs about the state, economy, and society (Kobrin 2004). In some countries, for instance, the government heavily regulates the processing of personal data, as data privacy is thought of as a matter of social protection. In other countries, however, data processing is rather lightly regulated to promote economic growth and innovation.

Not surprisingly, such jurisdictional incongruity and national differences tend to give rise to conflicts—as well as demand for cooperation—between jurisdictions. What happens when data flow between jurisdictions with different data laws and regulations? How do jurisdictions compete or cooperate over the flows of data between them? What courses of action can jurisdictions take to reconcile their differences while trying to have their preferences reflected in their respective regulatory policies? What implications does such "politics of data" have for the study of international relations?

This book purports to explore these questions by examining three high-profile cases of transatlantic conflict and cooperation concerning the transfer and use of personal data—the Safe Harbor arrangement, the passenger name record (PNR) dispute, and the Society for Worldwide Interbank Financial Transactions (SWIFT) affair.

Since the 1990s, the European Union (EU) and the United States (US) have had a series of talks over the transfer and use of personal data. The EU–US data negotiations began initially as a response to the 1995 EU Data Protection Directive, and in 2000 produced the Safe Harbor arrangement (later called the Safe Harbor framework) to ensure the continuity of commercial data flows from the jurisdiction of the EU to the US. Then, in the wake of the terrorist attacks of September 11, 2001, the transatlantic partners negotiated and concluded agreements to share information, including information related to individuals, for law enforcement purposes. In 2004, the EU and the US made an agreement to allow European airlines to provide air passenger information (i.e. PNR data) to the US Department of Homeland Security for the purposes of identifying terrorists and denying their entry into the country. Furthermore, the EU and the US struck a deal in 2009 to make the SWIFT company's financial transactions records available for the Terrorist Finance Tracking Program (TFTP) of the US Treasury Department.

These cases of EU–US data disputes are of empirical and theoretical interest for three reasons. First, they exemplify regulatory conflicts involving global regulatory powers. In the literature on the politics of regulation, the EU and the US are depicted as powers that have the capacity to set rules for international transactions, above all, by virtue of their sheer sizes (Drezner 2007; Bach and Newman 2007; Büthe and Mattli 2011). From this perspective, the transatlantic data conflicts can be seen as the cases in which the two regulatory powers competed to have their respective norms and interests reflected in the rules that would govern transactions of data between them. In this connection, it should be noted that data protection is one of the fields in which the EU has exerted global influence through its regulatory practices (Bach and Newman 2007).

Second, the cases provide examples of the politics of data privacy. Detailed analyses of the cases would show how the EU and the US, which have different substantive views on data privacy, have sought to reconcile the differences regarding the appropriate balance to be struck between data protection and other policy goals, such as economic growth and public security (Ryngaert 2015). Such inquiry is worthwhile, given that there has been considerable tension between data privacy and other interests. With the digitalization of the economy, business has increasingly needed to use personal data within and across borders. With the heightened threat of terrorism, on the other hand, there has been increasing demand to use personal data for law enforcement purposes within and between countries. These developments have further complicated the problem of using personal data without infringing on individuals' rights to privacy.

Finally, the cases illustrate the politics of extraterritorial regulation. A close examination of the cases would reveal how the beyond-the-border reach of one jurisdiction's regulations affects another jurisdiction's regulatory policy and practice, how conflicts might arise as a result of such extraterritorial exertion of regulatory authority, what responses the affected jurisdiction might possibly make, and how this type of regulatory conflict might be solved or managed. These questions are worth exploring in a world composed of sovereign states—which in principle claim authority within their territorially defined jurisdictions—but characterized by extensive interactions across borders—which both cause and result from globalization. Importantly, exploration of the politics of extraterritorial regulation could possibly make a contribution to the study of international relations, because "all matters of extraterritorial jurisdictional claims have consequences for international relations" (Kuner et al. 2013, p. 148).

Politics of Data Privacy

Data privacy is recognized as a legitimate concern in democratic countries around the world (Reidenberg 2000). At the same time, it is generally accepted that data privacy needs to be balanced against other social, economic, and political concerns, including commercial interests, economic as well as administrative efficiency, freedom of expression, and protection against crime (Raab 1999; Shaffer 2000).

The problem then is *how* to strike a balance between data privacy and other values and interests. This is a very difficult problem, to say the least. As Bennett and Raab point out, privacy is highly subjective and "[d]ifferent people may go about finding a balance in different ways, and arrive at different substantive points of reconciliation between competing values" (Bennett and Raab 2006, p. 13). So might different countries. The EU–US data disputes, indeed, signify the difficulty of striking a balance between data privacy and other important concerns.

Both the Safe Harbor arrangement and its successor, the Privacy Shield framework, can be seen as bargaining outcomes between the conflicting objectives of data privacy and commercial interests. The EU, with its emphasis on data privacy as a basic human right, insisted that an adequate level of protection should be provided to the data transferred from the EU to the US without disrupting transatlantic flows of data. The US, on the other hand, was driven more by economic interests and sought to minimize regulatory intervention in the market. So the Safe Harbor arrangement was made to respond to the EU's concern with the privacy of its citizens while also accommodating US (as well as European) commercial interests by ensuring the transferability of personal data from the EU to the US provided that certain data practices were restrained.

The PNR dispute and the SWIFT affair highlight the quandary of balancing data privacy concerns against public security concerns. In both cases, the main question was *how*—rather than *whether*—data containing personal information should be used in the US-led war on terrorism. More precisely, the question was how personal data held by private-sector entities should be utilized for law enforcement and counterterrorism activities.

The US government—and, to some extent, its EU counterparts—believed that use of PNR data was necessary to enhance border security, but the EU insisted that the personal data originating in the EU should be protected in the US in line with the European data protection standards. So the PNR agreements were concluded to facilitate the sharing of air passenger information under certain conditions to safeguard data privacy. More specifically, it was agreed that US authorities would receive fewer elements of PNR data than they wished, use the data received only for the purpose of counterterrorism, and retain the data for a shorter period of time than they wanted.

Similarly, the US government—and its EU counterparts—perceived the need to deploy financial transactions data to combat terrorist financing, but the EU demanded that the use of such data should be proportionate to the ends of counterterrorism—again in line with European data protection standards. So the TFTP agreement (also known as the SWIFT agreement) was sealed to make SWIFT data originating in the EU available to the TFTP with a set of guarantees and safeguards. Under the TFTP agreement, the US authorities would obtain limited sets of data, use them only for counterterrorism purposes, and retain them for a limited period of time.

It should be noted that, in all of the cases, the EU–US negotiations resulted in an agreement that in effect restricted US use of personal data originating in the EU. In short, the EU and the US tried to balance data privacy concerns against commercial or public security interests essentially by limiting the availability of personal data.

Politics of Extraterritorial Regulation

Acknowledging the relevance of the politics of data, this study is intended to add another dimension to the study of transatlantic data conflicts by assuming that the Safe Harbor arrangement, the PNR dispute, and the SWIFT affair represent cases of the politics of extraterritorial regulation. More precisely, it assumes that they are cases of extraterritoriality and what may be called "counter-extraterritoriality." In fact, all of the cases began with extraterritorial assertion of domestic or national regulations, followed by negotiations to manage cross-jurisdictional conflicts that arose from it, and resulted in arrangements that were intended to mitigate the impacts of extraterritorial regulations.

The negotiations leading to the Safe Harbor arrangement were prompted by the adoption of the EU Data Protection Directive, which contained extraterritorial clauses on data transfer to third countries (i.e. non-EU countries). From the viewpoint of the US, the extraterritorial reach of the EU regulation was a cause of concern not only because it could disrupt transatlantic data flows but also because it could affect the US privacy regime. So the Safe Harbor arrangement was made to allow the US to maintain its own privacy regime and thereby avoid the cost of making an internal adjustment (i.e. introducing European-style comprehensive privacy legislation) to meet the adequacy requirement of the EU directive's extraterritorial clause.

In contrast, the PNR dispute and the SWIFT affair grew out of the beyond-the-border reach of US counterterrorism regulation. While helping enhance border security, the use of PNR data for counterterrorism purposes might infringe the privacy right of air passengers. If EU citizens' right of privacy was undermined, furthermore, the effectiveness of the EU data protection regime would also be undermined. So the PNR agreements were negotiated to limit the negative impacts of US regulation by specifying the condition of data sharing. Similarly, while it assisted in combating terrorist financing, the use of SWIFT data might violate the privacy right of EU citizens whose financial transaction records were made available to US authorities. So the TFTP agreement was made to prevent "disproportionate and excessive" use of data originating in the EU by US authorities and thus protect the integrity of the EU data privacy regime.

Until recently, "[e]xtraterritorial regulation has received almost no attention from international relations scholars, although it has long been of theoretical and practical interest to international lawyers" (Putnam 2009, p. 469). While a relatively small literature on the international politics of extraterritoriality now exists, these studies primarily focus on the extraterritorial acts of the "most assertive" state—that is, the US (Putnam 2009; Raustiala 2009; Kaczmarek and Newman 2011). However, the US is not the only country that has claimed extraterritorial regulatory authority. Most notably, the EU, the other global regulatory power (Drezner 2007; Bach and Newman 2007), has actively employed extraterritoriality in recent years and exerted considerable influence over regulatory policies in other jurisdictions.

Furthermore, focusing on the acts of the "dominant" power, the existing studies tend to downplay the reaction to the extraterritorial reach of regulatory authority. Yet "counter-extraterritoriality" is an integral part of the politics of extraterritoriality. Indeed, the EU–US data disputes can be seen as cases of extraterritoriality *and* counter-extraterritoriality in which the two regulatory powers switched their positions, so to speak; while the US countered the EU's extraterritorial regulatory reach in the Safe Harbor case, the EU countered US extraterritorial claims in the PNR and SWIFT cases. Were the EU and US practices of regulatory extraterritoriality based on the same logic? Did the EU and the US counter the claim of extraterritorial regulatory authority in the same fashion? What was the outcome? These questions are to be answered by the case studies.

It should be emphasized that the politics of extraterritoriality may be as interactive as other aspects of international politics. The interactive nature of the politics of extraterritoriality was evident even in the cases of the PNR dispute and the SWIFT affair, which are, according to a prevailing view, instances of hegemonic behaviors by the US (Klosek 2007). It has been argued that transatlantic security cooperation is characterized by an asymmetrical relationship, in which the EU adopts norms and policies that the US unilaterally promotes (Argomaniz 2009). Equating extraterritoriality with dominance, however, such a conceptualization of US assertiveness tends to obscure the fact that the EU had modest, if not huge, success in having its data protection standards reflected in the agreements with the US (Newman 2008b, 2010, 2011; de Goede 2012a; Suda 2013). Given the priority placed on counterterrorism in post-9/11 America, it is noteworthy that the EU gained concessions from the US with regard to the transfer and use of data that might be of significant value to enhancing border security and tracking terrorist activities.

Transatlantic Data Disputes: An Overview

The Safe Harbor Arrangement

The EU–US negotiations that led to the Safe Harbor arrangement of 2000 began in conjunction with the adoption of the EU Data Protection Directive in 1995. The directive provided, among other things, that personal data could be transferred to a third country only when the third country in question ensures an "adequate level of protection" of personal data. As the US data privacy regime was substantially different from the EU's and appeared to fail to meet the adequacy criteria, the extraterritorial clause of the EU directive could disrupt data flows from the jurisdiction of the EU to the US. To avoid such disruption, the EU and the US agreed that those US firms that pledged to comply with a set of data privacy principles (Safe Harbor principles) would be deemed to provide an "adequate level of protection" and could receive personal data from the EU territory (Swire and Litan 1998; Charlesworth 2000; Farrrell 2003, 2005; Newman 2008b).

Recently, the Safe Harbor was replaced by a new framework called "Privacy Shield" as a result of the revelation of the scandal involving the US National Security Agency (NSA). In essence, the Privacy Shield framework is an updated version of the Safe Harbor arrangement, designed to allow continued flow of data across the Atlantic while complying with the legal requirement of the Data Protection Directive.

The PNR dispute

Initially, the EU–US data talks were held in the context of the development of the information-based economy in general and the emergence of electronic commerce in particular. The terrorist attacks of September 11, 2001, fundamentally changed the context of the EU–US data talks. While the Safe Harbor arrangement was made to construct an international foundation of electronic commerce (Farrell 2003), the transfer and use of PNR data emerged as "one of the most controversial issues in the transatlantic security relationship" (Argomaniz 2009, p. 120).

In the wake of the September 11 attacks, the US Department of Homeland Security began to require operators of all US-bound passenger air flights, including those from Europe, to submit PNR data for the purposes of identifying terrorists and denying their entry into the country. Since PNR data contained the personal information of passengers, consistency between the US requirement and the EU Data Protection Directive came into question. To find a legal solution, the EU and the US in 2004 made an agreement that would allow European airlines to provide PNR data to the Department of Homeland Security on condition that the data provided were adequately handled. However, the European Court of Justice nullified this agreement, and, as a consequence, a new PNR deal was struck in 2007. In 2012, the PNR agreement was once again revised to obtain consent from the European Parliament (Heisenberg 2005; Hailbronner et al. 2008; Argomaniz 2009; Pawlak 2009; Newman 2008b, 2010, 2011; Suda 2013).

The SWIFT Affair

The SWIFT affair also was fallout from US counterterrorism efforts. Shortly after the terrorist attacks of September 11, the US Treasury Department began to issue administrative orders to the SWIFT company, instructing SWIFT to make the financial transactions records it possessed available for the TFTP. Once the existence of this clandestine operation was revealed, it provoked a fierce reaction in the EU as SWIFT's financial transactions data contained personal information of payers and recipients, including those residing within the EU. In response, the Treasury Department in 2007 gave "guarantees" about the use of data received from SWIFT. The EU and the US eventually agreed on a legal framework for the transfer of SWIFT data from Europe to the US that detailed the handling and use of the data obtained from SWIFT. Sealed in the spirit of transatlantic partnership, however, the TFTP agreement was highly controversial and was rejected by the European Parliament. Upon renegotiation, a new agreement was finally reached in 2010 (de Goede 2012a; Suda 2013).

It should be noted that both the TFTP and PNR agreements were negotiated to facilitate the cross-border sharing of information held by the private sector with a view to enhancing counterterrorism cooperation. In other words, the TFTP and PNR cases illustrate the growing interaction between public and private sectors in the processing of personal data as well as increase in data sharing between states. Such interaction reflects a trend that, in this age of advanced information communication technology, private entities, such as airlines and financial institutions, hold a vast amount of information that may be valuable for law enforcement or national security.

Plan of the Book

This book has nine chapters. Chapter 1 discusses the general issues of the politics of data privacy. It elucidates the intricate policy problem of balancing data privacy against other important concerns, particularly commercial interests and public security concerns.

Chapter 2 deals with the logic of extraterritoriality and counter-extraterritoriality. The first half of this chapter discusses different forms of extraterritoriality and the rationale behind such expansive claims of regulatory authority. The second half of the chapter deals with the logic of counter-extraterritoriality, which is the reverse of the logic of extraterritoriality, and possible responses to extraterritoriality.

Chapter 3 discusses the EU Data Protection Directive, with a focus on its extraterritorial implications, as a background to the cases. The General Data Protection Regulation, which is currently replacing the 1995 Directive, will be also discussed.

Chapter 4 provides an account of the Safe Harbor negotiations between the US and the EU, and the resulting arrangement. It examines how the EU regulation based on the Data Protection Directive spilled (or could spill) over into the US and how the US (together with the EU) dealt with this regulatory spillover. The chapter also discusses the effect of the NSA scandal on transatlantic data politics and the establishment of the Privacy Shield framework.

Chapter 5 presents a case study of the EU–US row over the transfer and use of PNR data. It examines how the post-9/11 US counterterrorism regulation concerning air passenger information affected (or might affect) the privacy of EU citizens as well as the European data protection regime, how the EU responded to such extraterritorial reach of US regulatory authority, how the EU and the US negotiated a series of agreements on the transfer and use of the PNR data originating in the EU, and what the PNR agreements mean to the transatlantic politics of data.

Chapter 6 examines the development of the EU's PNR policy, which culminated in the adoption of the EU PNR Directive in 2016. Particular attention will be paid to the influence of the EU–US PNR negotiations and the resulting agreements on the proposed introduction of the EU's own PNR system.

Chapter 7 presents a case study of the EU–US controversy over the transfer and use of financial transaction data held by SWIFT. It examines what impact the TFTP in the US had (or might have) on the data privacy of EU citizens as well as the European data protection regime, how the EU reacted to the beyond-the-border effect of US counterterrorism operations, how the EU and the US managed the friction through negotiations, and what the TFTP agreement denotes in the context of the politics of data transfer.

Chapter 8 discusses how issues related to data privacy have been addressed in recent negotiations of mega-free trade agreements (FTAs), namely the Transatlantic Trade and Investment Partnership (TTIP) agreement and the Trans-Pacific Partnership (TPP) agreement. These cases are important, because they demonstrate how the issues of data protection and privacy may be intertwined with FTAs.

Chapter 9 concludes the study with discussion of the findings from the cases. It also discusses the significance of territoriality as an implication of the cases for the study of international relations.

1 The Politics of Data Privacy

Data privacy is an elusive concept, but as a policy problem it basically revolves around the issue of how to protect personal data without unduly restricting its use or, conversely, how to use personal data without infringing the data subject's (individual's) right to privacy. The challenge of the data privacy policy, therefore, concerns striking a balance between the protection of personal data and the use of such data. However, there is no universally defined point at which these two potentially conflicting policy objectives are balanced. Rather, the way in which a balance is struck depends on each country's (or people's) social, economic, cultural, and other values and interests.

Data Privacy as a Policy Problem

In relation to personal data, privacy (or data privacy) refers to an individual's right to be able to control information that relates to him or herself. Data protection, a term derived from the German word *Datenschutz*, is used in much the same way as privacy in the above sense (Bennett and Raab 2006).[1]

There is widespread recognition at least in democratic countries that data privacy needs to be protected (Reidenberg 2000). Indeed, virtually all liberal-democratic states have some form of privacy or data protection laws. In Europe, Sweden led the way and passed its Data Protection Act in 1973; subsequently, West Germany enacted its Federal Data Protection Act in 1977, before France, Norway, Denmark, Austria, the United Kingdom, and other European countries followed suit. In North America, the United States (US) enacted its Privacy Act in 1974 and Canada passed its Personal Information Protection and Electronic Documents Act in 2002. In Asia, South Korea passed its Data Protection Act in 2001 and Japan enacted its Act on the Protection of Personal Information in 2003 (Greenleaf 2013; Gellman and Dixon 2011).

It should be noted that, whatever the name of its governing legislation, data privacy law—and regulation based on it—is about defining, in one way or another, the limits of the processing and use of personal data (Bennett and Raab 2006). For instance, one of the fundamental privacy principles is that data collected for one purpose should not be used for other purposes without the consent of the data subject. In essence, protection of data privacy necessitates *some* restriction on the use of personal information.

Data privacy law and regulation do not impose total prohibition on the use of personal data because there is need to use such data for economic, social, or other benefits. For instance, personal information is widely used in a variety of business activities. Electronic commerce, for example, cannot be carried out without using consumers' personal data (such as names, addresses, telephone numbers, credit card numbers, and email addresses). However, the use of personal data is not confined to digital transactions. Non-tech companies also routinely use personal data for marketing, intra-corporate management, and other day-to-day operations. Furthermore, personal data is commonly and increasingly used by public authorities for purposes ranging from the provision of social welfare services, to taxation, and to law enforcement. The rise of "e-government" accelerates this trend. Data privacy law and regulation, therefore, generally allows—even facilitates—the use of personal data while restraining certain data practices to reduce potential harm to individuals (Raab 1999; Bennett and Raab 2006).

In short, data privacy in law and practice pursues two potentially conflicting objectives: protection of personal data and "fair" use of such data. As such, the data privacy policy seeks to strike a balance between competing values and interests typically by regulating how and when personal data should be available, or not available, to accommodate economic, social, or administrative needs. However, "what is acceptable in one country might not do in another" (Raab 1999, p. 73). Countries (or people) differ from one another in their social norms, cultural traditions, political philosophy, historical experience, economic circumstances, and other policy backgrounds. Consequently, there are substantial differences in data privacy law and regulation between countries; even between the US and European countries that share fundamental values.

Data Privacy and Free Flows of Data

At the international level, the problem of striking a balance between data privacy and other concerns may be transposed as a problem of striking a balance between privacy protection and the facilitation of the movement and use of data across national borders. How can personal data be protected when transferred and used across borders? Conversely, how can personal data be transferred and used across borders without infringing the data subject's right to privacy? These questions were first raised in the 1970s in response to computerization and the growth of transnational use of personal data for commercial and economic purposes. Today, they are even more crucial as the increased global integration of the economy and the advent of the global network of networks, that is, the internet, have resulted in exponential increase in transborder data flows (Kuner 2013).

In an information-based and globalizing economy, personal data collected in one country may well be transferred to and used in another country. For example, cross-border movement of information about individual customers is essential for business operations of firms in some sectors (e.g. financial services and tourism); so is transborder movement of personal information about employees for intra-corporation management of transnational corporations (e.g. processing payrolls). Presumably, the fewer—regulatory, technological or other—barriers to the use and movement of personal data, the more efficient transnational economic activities would be.

If given free rein, however, firms may be inclined to develop privacy-invasive practices. For example, firms may evade the strict privacy regulation of one country by transferring data to another country with lax or no privacy regulation (i.e. a so-called "data haven") and processing data there. In other words, firms may be tempted to take advantage of differences in data protection regulation between jurisdictions. To prevent such practices there needs to be some rules to govern the transfer and use of personal information across borders at national and/or international level.

Privacy and business interests, nonetheless, are not necessarily incompatible with each other. It may be in the interests of business to protect their customers' data to the extent that the protection of personal data is required to build trust and confidence in commercial transactions. Indeed, without trust and confidence in transactions it would be difficult to promote economic activities that rely on data flows (e.g. electronic commerce).

OECD Privacy Guidelines and CoE Convention No. 108

While, at present, no global framework exists to govern data privacy, international attempts to reconcile privacy concerns and economic needs are notably found in the Organisation for Economic Co-operation and Development (OECD) Guidelines on the Protection of Privacy and Transborder Flows of Personal Data (OECD Privacy Guidelines),[2] and the Council of Europe's (CoE) 1981 Convention for the Protection of Individuals with regard to Automatic Processing of Personal Data (Convention No. 108).[3]

The OECD Privacy Guidelines, a leading example of an international framework for privacy, were originally adopted in 1980 with the recognition that "[m]ember countries have a common interest … in reconciling fundamental but competing values such as privacy and the free flow of information." Convention No. 108, another important international framework for data privacy, was also enacted in recognition of the necessity "to reconcile the fundamental values of the respect for privacy and the free flow of information between peoples" (Preamble).

The OECD Privacy Guidelines and Convention No. 108 are viewed as providing a fundamental framework to protect personal information

(Hurley and Mayer-Schönberger 2000). In particular, the OECD Privacy Guidelines have been accepted by a broad range of industrial countries, including the US and the member states of the European Union (EU), which together have the lion's share of the development and use of information systems. However, neither the OECD Privacy Guidelines nor Convention No. 108 specifies precisely how countries should strike a balance between data privacy and other interests (especially economic interests). Rather, they establish a set of general principles to harmonize national privacy laws and regulations. The assumption is twofold: if countries follow common privacy principles, a sufficient level of data protection will be provided across all the subscribing countries, and if equivalently sufficient levels of protection are provided, data should be allowed to flow freely between these countries.

In the OECD Guidelines, OECD countries are recommended to implement in their domestic legislation the following eight data protection principles.[4]

- Collection limitation principle: there should be limits to the collection of personal data and any such data should be obtained by lawful and fair means and, where appropriate, with the knowledge or consent of the data subject (i.e. individual).
- Data quality principle: personal data should be relevant to the purposes for which they are to be used, and, to the extent necessary for those purposes, should be accurate, complete, and kept up-to-date.
- Purpose specification principle: the purposes for which personal data are collected should be specified not later than at the time of data collection and the subsequent use limited to the fulfillment of those purposes or such others as are not incompatible with those purposes and as are specified on each occasion of change of purpose.
- Use limitation principle: personal data should not be disclosed, made available or otherwise used for purposes other than those specified except with the consent of the data subject or by the authority of law.
- Security safeguards principle: personal data should be protected by reasonable security safeguards against such risks as loss or unauthorized access, destruction, use, modification, or disclosure of data.
- Openness principle: there should be a general policy of openness about developments, practices and policies with respect to personal data; means should be readily available to establish the existence and nature of personal data, and the main purposes of their use, as well as the identity and usual residence of the data (e.g. firm).
- Individual participation principle: an individual should have the right to know whether or not the data controller has data relating to him or her, the right to have the data relating to him or her communicated, the right to be given reasons if a request for communication is denied,

the right to challenge data relating to her, and the right to have the data erased, rectified, completed, or amended.

- Accountability principle: a data controller should be accountable for complying with measures which give effect to the principles stated above.

Assuming that these domestic implementation guidelines are followed, it is then recommended that the member countries "endeavour to remove or avoid creating, in the name of privacy protection, unjustified obstacles to transborder flows of personal data."

Similarly, Convention No. 108 requires each member state to take necessary measures in its domestic law to give effect to the basic principles for the data protection it stipulates. For example, it provides that, in relation to the quality of data, personal data undergoing automatic processing shall be: (a) obtained and processed fairly and lawfully; (b) stored for specified and legitimate purposes and not used in a way incompatible with those purposes; (c) adequate, relevant and not excessive in relation to the purposes for which they are stored; (d) accurate and, where necessary, kept up to date; (e) preserved in a form which permits identification of the data subjects for no longer than is required for the purpose for which those data are stored (Article 5). The convention then provides that "[a] Party shall not, for the sole purpose of the protection of privacy, prohibit or subject to special authorisation transborder flows of personal data going to the territory of another Party" (Article 12).

It should be noted that, in both the OECD Guidelines and Convention No. 108, privacy principles are to be implemented by each state in their domestic context of particular social, cultural, and other values and interests. As a result, there remain—rather than being dissolved—"disparities in national legislations"[5] on data privacy. This means that tension may arise between countries with different data protection law and regulation when personal data flow across their borders.

Data Privacy and Public Security

As noted, the problem of data privacy was set on the international agenda with the increase in transborder movement and use of personal data for commercial and economic purposes. In recent years, data privacy has become an even more salient issue internationally in the context of law enforcement and public security.

Personal information is widely used for the purposes of law enforcement. Investigation of crimes, for example, cannot be conducted without the use of personally identifiable information. Arguably, the more access law enforcement agencies have to personal information, the more efficient would be their efforts to deal with and prevent crimes. It may even be argued that privacy is not an absolute right and that individuals' right to data privacy should be overridden by public safety considerations. From the perspective of data privacy, however, there should be certain limits on the use of personal information for public security purposes.

Tension between data privacy and public security is not new. The encryption debate in the 1990s provides an example of such a tense relationship (Deibert 2002). Encryption is a very powerful tool to secure electronic communications from unauthorized access and thereby protect an individual's right to privacy (Reitinger 2000). However, making encryption products widely available may compromise public or national security because it grants the same level of security to the communication of criminals, terrorists, and foreign intelligence agents (Bessette and Haufler 2001). In other words, the spread of encryption technology and products could be detrimental to public security as they might hamper information gathering by national security and law enforcement authorities.[6]

More recently, use of personal data for public security purposes has been under intensive debate in connection with counterterrorism and surveillance activities. Critics claim that, after the terrorist attacks of September 11, 2001, the world witnessed the general erosion of individual privacy rights (e.g. Klosek 2007). The USA PATRIOT[7] Act of 2001 is perhaps the most prominent example of the expansion of government surveillance authorities after 9/11 (Rotenberg 2003). US (and other states') government authorities, in fact, now not only gather information directly but also tap the data collected and held by the private sector (such as individuals' records on travel, financial transactions, and electronic communication) for counterterrorism and law enforcement purposes. Even in Europe, which is said to be especially sensitive to the potential harm of large-scale collection of records about individuals due to its historical experiences (Hurley and Mayer-Schönberger 2000), the EU enacted the Data Retention Directive in 2007, requiring member countries to mandate the retention by telecommunications companies of records of the sender, recipient, and time of communication, so that law enforcement authorities can use the data when necessary (Roberts and Palfrey 2010). Such interaction between the public and private sectors is one of the developments that have significantly affected the politics of data privacy.

Importantly, in the age of globalization, the use of personal data for public security purposes almost inevitably has an international dimension. This is particularly the case with counterterrorism. Nowadays, terrorism has an increasingly transnational nature as terrorists exploit the seamless flows of goods, money, services, and persons across borders. Accordingly, the "exchange of operational information, especially regarding actions or movements of terrorist persons or networks"[8] has become an integral part of international efforts to prevent and suppress terrorism. In other words, gathering and sharing of information, including that related to individuals, is a vital component of international counterterrorism cooperation.

The problem from the standpoint of civil liberty is that governments may promote such information gathering and sharing at the expense of the data privacy rights of individuals. How can personal information be shared for public security purposes without infringing the individual's right to privacy? Conversely, how can data privacy be protected when personal data are shared between law enforcement agencies of different countries? In this connection, it should be noted that one country's data privacy policy may have an effect on another country's efforts to gather information, because data privacy in practice means placing *some* limits on the availability of personal data.

The existing international frameworks for data privacy do not address the tension between individual privacy and public safety. The OECD Privacy Guidelines make "national sovereignty, national security and public policy" exceptions to the application of the basic privacy principles (Part I).[9] Likewise, Convention No. 108 provides that derogation from the data protection principles are allowed where this "constitutes a necessary measure in a democratic society in the interests of … protecting State security, public safety, the monetary interests of the State or the suppression of criminal offences" (Article 9). Public safety is simply beyond the scope of these international frameworks.

Each government, therefore, must strike a balance between privacy concerns and public security interests in light of the particular values and beliefs of the domestic society. Here, once again, what is acceptable in one country might not be so in another. When substantial difference exists in the way different concerns are balanced, information sharing becomes difficult even between countries that have common interests in countering terrorism and enhancing national security—as is the case with the US and the EU.

Conclusion

In a networked world, where massive amount of data, including personal data, are transferred and used across borders, data privacy is an inherently international or transnational problem. Nevertheless, the essence of data privacy as an international policy problem is the intricate task of balancing data privacy concern against other needs. It is widely accepted that data privacy should be balanced against economic interests; the two major international accords on data privacy, the OECD Privacy Guidelines and Convention No. 108, endorse this view. Furthermore, protection of personal data should be balanced against public security interests, both nationally and internationally. It would not be an exaggeration to say that, under the shadow of the war on terrorism, the question of the balance between privacy and public security is more critical than ever before.

In general, the balance between data privacy and other concerns is struck in the context of social, cultural, economic, and political values and interests, which may differ between societies (or people) as well as from time to time. In other words, countries may differ from one another in the perceived balance between competing objectives. Such differences may be reflected in national laws and regulatory policies and, with the transborder flows of data, may cause legal or regulatory conflicts between jurisdictions. In fact, the EU–US data disputes can be seen as being derived from differences in the emphasis that the transatlantic partners placed—for good reason—on different aspects of the data problem.

It is important to note that the difference in data privacy policy across countries—embodied in their data privacy law and regulation—matters, because of personal data flows between them. In the presence of transborder data flows, the data privacy policy of one country may have a detrimental effect on the privacy rights of individuals in another country, just as the data privacy policy of one country may affect flows of data from and to another country. Such beyond-the-border effects are at the core of the contemporary politics of data privacy as well as the politics of extraterritorial regulation, which will be discussed in the next chapter.

Notes

1 It should be noted that "privacy" is a broader interest than "data privacy" (or "information privacy") and includes the protection of such interests as bodily integrity, solitude, and freedom from observation (Greenleaf 2013). In other words, what is called "data privacy" (or "information privacy") is a particular aspect of privacy (Bennett and Raab 2006).

2 The OECD was established in 1961 by twenty countries in Europe and North America with the aims of promoting policies designed to achieve high economic growth in the member countries and to contribute to the development of the world economy (Convention on the Organisation for Economic Co-operation and Development, Article 1).

3 The Council of Europe was established in 1949 by ten European countries with the aims of promoting human rights, democracy, and the rule of law throughout its member states.

4 These eight principles were maintained as they were when the guidelines were updated in 2013, as the expert group that drafted the updated guidelines took the view that the balance reflected in the eight basic principles of the OECD's 1980 Guidelines remains generally sound and should be preserved (Supplementary explanatory memorandum to the revised recommendation of the council concerning guidelines governing the protection of privacy and transborder flows of personal data 2013).

5 The OECD Privacy Guidelines were formulated to address concerns that "disparities in national legislations"—especially the differences between American privacy legislation and European data protection laws—"could hamper the free flow of personal data across frontiers" (Preface). According to Michael Kirby, who chaired the OECD expert group that drafted the Privacy Guidelines, the OECD concern—or rather non-European countries' concern—"was that the responses of European nations (and European regional institutions) to the challenges of TBDF [transborder data flows] for privacy might potentially erect legal and economic barriers." The US was particularly concerned with the possibility that "restrictions on these flows could cause serious disruption in important sectors of the economy, such as banking and insurance" (Preface) because it was "the largest player in the processing of automated data (including for airlines, hotels, business, insurance, and banking information)" (Kirby 2011, p. 8).

6 The US government was particularly concerned with this possibility, and proposed systems through which law enforcement authorities could decrypt and gain access to suspect communications. This proposal, however, was eventually defeated by vehement opposition from a coalition of civil liberty and business interests (Bessette and Haufler 2001).

7 USA PATRIOT is an abbreviation of "Uniting and Strengthening America by Providing Appropriate Tools Required to Intercept and Obstruct Terrorism."

8 United Nations Security Council Resolution 1373, September 28, 2001.

9 At the same time, the OECD Privacy Guidelines provide that such exceptions should be (a) as few as possible, and (b) made known to the public.

2 The Politics of Extraterritorial Regulation

Data privacy is only one of the issues on the policy agenda in the interdependent world, where goods, services, money, people, and information flow across national borders. These flows, indeed, can raise a problem because their effects on the domestic society may not only be positive but also negative. For instance, while trade generally improves the welfare of people, trafficking of drugs, arms, or child pornography—typical examples of transnational crime—does harm to it.

Thus, governments may find it necessary to harness or regulate transborder flows in an effort to reduce harmful effects arising from them. However, regulation of transborder flows is often difficult, not least because the reach of national regulation is incongruent with the scope of what is being regulated.

One way to deal with this incongruence is simply to extend the reach of national regulation beyond the territorial boundaries of the state. Extraterritorial regulation, however, can have a "spillover" effect and cause friction between the regulating state and the affected state. This is particularly the case when the former demands policy change in the latter, thereby forcing it to bear the cost of policy adjustment.

Logic of Extraterritoriality

In practice, extraterritoriality refers to the exercise of direct authority over entities and behaviors in foreign jurisdictions (Raustiala 2009; Putnam 2009).[1] Such transborder claims of authority represent a violation of—or at least an exception to—the sovereign principle of territoriality. In the modern world, a sovereign state exercises its authority within a demarcated space—that is, within its own territory (Agnew 1994)—and such authoritative control over behavior within a delimited boundary is assumed to be a major dimension of territoriality (Kahler 2006). Nonetheless, extraterritorial claims increasingly have been made in a variety of areas, including anti-trust, securities exchange, intellectual property, criminal law, the environment, labor, narcotics trafficking, and money laundering (Putnam 2009; Kaczmarek and Newman 2011).

Extraterritoriality Based on Nationality

Extraterritoriality takes different forms. In some cases, an extraterritorial claim is made by asserting jurisdiction over a person—whether a natural or legal person—inside the territory of another state. This kind of extraterritoriality has a long history, with diplomatic law being one common example (Kaczmarek and Newman 2011).[2]

In recent years, however, extraterritoriality is more often than not employed as a means of regulating activities taking place in a foreign jurisdiction. An example is provided by foreign bribery regulation, which criminalizes the bribery of foreign public officials by a firm and/or person engaging in international business transactions. In one instance, the United States (US) Foreign Corrupt Practices Act (FCPA) was enforced against an American firm, namely IBM, for bribing Argentine government officials when it was trying to obtain a business contract in Argentina (Darrough 2010). Likewise, Japan's Law to Prevent Unfair Competition was applied to prosecute a Japanese consultant company that had made a corrupt payment to Vietnamese public officials when doing business related to official development assistance (ODA) in Vietnam (*Asahi Shimbun* 2008).

It should be noted that such exercise of extraterritorial jurisdiction relies on the very fact that the firm and/or person committing the criminal offense in question is a national of the regulating state. In this sense, this sort of extraterritoriality is claimed on the basis of the tie of nationality rather than territorial connection.

Extraterritorial Regulation of Transactional Conduct

Extraterritorial effects also arise from the application of domestic law and regulation to activities taking place across jurisdictions. This application typically involves the imposition of over-the-border obligations on transnational actors. For example, the US currently plans to require that 100 percent of US-bound cargo containers be scanned at foreign seaports under the Security and Accountability for Every (SAFE) Port Act of 2006 (Caldwell 2008). If implemented, this measure will have considerable effect on foreign exporters because they may have to bear the cost of scanning equipment as well as the cost of personnel to operate it. The US government's requirement to submit passenger name record (PNR) data provides another example of a transboundary regulatory obligation. Under the US Aviation Act, non-US air carriers (along with US-based carriers) are subject to this regulation so long as they operate flights arriving and departing from the US.

It is noteworthy that, as the cases above imply, this type of extraterritorial regulation is based on the territorial connection to the regulatory state of the entities that engage in transnational conduct. That is to say, domestic regulatory rules can be imposed on foreign ships or air carriers because a part of their transactions is conducted within the territory of the regulating state.

This suggests that territoriality still matters significantly in the globalizing world. In a recent example, non-European Union (EU) airlines (along with EU airlines) are required to participate in the EU Emissions Trading System (ETS), which was launched in 2005 and expanded in 2008 to include *all* flights from, to, and within the European Economic Area (EEA)[3] (European Commission 2014). Here, the physical, albeit transient, presence of non-EU airlines in the European market brings them within the reach of the EU regulation.

Extraterritoriality Based on "Effects"

Finally, extraterritoriality occurs when domestic law and regulation are directly applied to entities and their behaviors *regardless of their country of origin or the location of the conduct*. This relatively "new" version of extraterritoriality was pioneered in the US after World War I, but it has spread to other countries and regions, including Canada, the United Kingdom, Australia, France, Germany, Japan, South Korea, and, increasingly, the EU (Kaczmarek and Newman 2011; Putnam 2009).

The logic of such extraterritorial extension of authority is rather straightforward. In a world of cross-border transactions, states seek to reduce negative effects arising from activities in other jurisdictions on their respective territories (Raustiala 2009). Here, extraterritorial jurisdiction is justified as a means by which states mitigate or manage negative effects (or negative externalities) from foreign jurisdictions.

Examples of effects-based extraterritoriality are abundantly found in the area of competition policy (Devuyst 2000). Most prominently, the US has applied its anti-competitive laws to mergers undertaken partially or fully outside its territorial boundary since the landmark *Alcoa* case.[4] The reasoning is, as the US court decided, "acts that had tangible impacts within its borders could be regulated by the United States, wherever they might have originated" (Raustiala 2009, p. 95). More recently, the EU too has been active in regulating mergers planned in third countries (Scott 2014a). In *Gencor vs. the European Commission*, for example, the European Commission raised an objection to a merger between South African platinum companies, arguing that the concentration deal would result in a platinum duopoly and have an adverse effect on EU consumers (Broberg 2000).

However, there is more to negative externalities than mere infringement of interests of domestic entities. According to Putnam's study of US law practices (2009), extraterritoriality is employed when external conduct threatens to undercut the operation or integrity of domestic legal and regulatory regimes, broadly defined. This "domestic integrity argument" can be found in numerous cases of US extraterritorial regulatory practices. For instance, US insider trading regulation can be applied extraterritorially, not only to protect ordinary investors from the harmful effects of "material, non-public information" about securities but also to safeguard the US financial regulatory regime. The point is that the efficiency of US insider trading regulation would be compromised if corporate insiders could circumvent prosecution simply by undertaking the prohibited activities outside the territory of the US (Bach and Newman 2010). The extraterritorial enforcement of FCPA presumably is based on the same reasoning, although it also has been intended to safeguard US firms from "unfair" competition with foreign rivals that engage in "corrupt practices" (Kaczmarek and Newman 2011).

The "domestic integrity" argument can also be seen in the extraterritorial practices of the EU. For example, the EU's regulation on derivatives (European Market Instrument Regulation, EMIR) imposes clearing and risk-mitigating obligations on persons concluding certain types of derivative contracts, even when the contract in question is concluded exclusively between third-country entities. This requirement is not only to protect EU persons from financial risks but also to prevent the regulatory authority of the EU from being undermined by measures taken by individuals to evade obligations imposed by EU law (Scott 2014a). The rationale behind the extraterritorial application of EU data privacy regulations is in a similar vein. Article 25 of the 1995 Data Protection Directive (95/46/EC) explicitly requires that personal data be transferred to a third country only when the country in question provides an "adequate level of protection" of such data, not only to protect EU citizens from potential abuse of personal data but also to protect the integrity of the EU data regime.

It should be stressed that, logically, such effects-based extraterritoriality is employed when states have divergent policy preferences and practices.[5] Hypothetically, if all countries have anti-corruption or anti-trust laws with equivalent provisions and enforce them to an equal extent, the US (or any other country) would not have an incentive to extend the reach of its foreign bribery regulation or competition policy. In this light, extraterritoriality can be considered a unilateral effort to manage differences in law and regulation across jurisdictions (Raustiala 2009).[6]

Sources of Extraterritorial Assertion of Regulatory Authority

As noted, extraterritoriality is now becoming a global phenomenon. At the same time, "[s]tate capacity to enforce domestic laws extraterritorially varies widely" (Putnam 2009, p. 483). What then accounts for the variance in the *effective* extraterritorial assertion of regulatory authority?

Market Power

In the realm of market-related regulation, regulators often leverage *access* to the domestic or internal market to gain actual influence on foreign or transactional conduct. For example, if a cargo container ship refuses to comply with the requirement of the SAFE Port Act, it would potentially be denied access to US ports and consequently the vast US market. By the same token, an air carrier that refuses to participate in the EU ETS could technically be excluded from the lucrative European air-transport service market. To take another example, the wielding of access to the US financial market (and, by implication, the vital US clearing system) has been a key feature of US efforts to control money laundering in foreign jurisdictions that may be adverse to the interests of the US.[7] In short, market access can be used as clout to extend the reach of regulation beyond borders.

This observation is consistent with the "market power" argument of realist strain made in the literature on the politics of regulation. According to Drezner (2007), a state with a significantly large domestic market is able to impose its regulatory preferences on other states by using the "threat of complete or partial market closure" (p. 32). Here, market size matters as the cost of exclusion is in proportion to the size of the market. It would be highly costly, indeed, to be excluded from the market of such "economic great powers" as the US or the EU.[8] To the extent that it is backed by market power, it can be argued that effective extraterritorial regulation tends to be a privilege of large countries.

However, it may be the *presence* in the market of a foreign entity that could make it vulnerable to extraterritorial regulation. For example, the US Securities and Exchange Commission (SEC) could bring a claim against Siemens AG, a German engineering firm, for making dubious payments to foreign government officials in at least ten countries, including Argentina, Bangladesh, China, Israel, Mexico, Nigeria, Russia, and Vietnam, because the company had listed its stock on the New York Stock Exchange and was an SEC registrant. Since Siemens registered with SEC, furthermore, the US Department of Justice (DOJ) could prosecute Siemens for fraudulent books and records (Darrough 2010).[9] In this case, the foreign firm fell within the purview of US regulatory authorities because it took advantage of the US financial market.

Domestic presence makes foreign entities especially vulnerable when the holding of assets is involved. According to Raustiala (2009), the US experience suggests that the presence of a valuable asset (e.g. a bank deposit) within the territory makes the holder of the asset vulnerable to extraterritorial enforcement of domestic law and regulation because such an asset can be sanctioned (e.g. frozen or seized) by domestic regulators or courts. Raustiala describes the nexus of the gravitational effect of a large market, presence in the market, and vulnerability to extraterritorial regulation as follows:

> Because its economic power was so great foreign firms found the American market irresistible. But their entry into the American market created legal vulnerability, because it was the presence of assets within the reach of federal courts that generally gave the new extraterritoriality its practical bite.
>
> (Raustiala 2009, p. 95)

The recent rise of the EU as an extraterritorial regulator is also backed by market power; the EU does have a large internal market. However, it is rather difficult to argue that the effectiveness of the extraterritorial assertion of EU regulation is always derived from the sheer size of its internal market. This difficulty particularly exists with financial regulation. The EU is not dominant in the finance sector to the same extent as the US, which dominates the world's financial transactions by virtue of the size, efficiency, and internationalization of its domestic financial market (Simmons 2001). Likewise, it is hard to maintain that the effectiveness of extraterritorial assertion of EU data protection regulation is founded on the power of its digital (e.g. electronic commerce) market, which is relatively limited in size (Bach and Newman 2007).

Regulatory Capacity

While market power is an important element of extraterritoriality, the effective assertion of extraterritorial authority generally requires a certain level of institutional capacity. To begin with, an assertive state must have the capacity to formulate regulatory rules, because "[o]ne needs a regulation to apply it extraterritorially" (Raustiala 2009, p. 119).[10] In addition, an assertive state must have regulators with expertise and, importantly, statutory sanctioning power to enforce and monitor regulation. In short, effective regulation requires what Bach and Newman (2007) call "regulatory capacity."

According to Bach and Newman (2007), the EU's growing international regulatory influence in such fields as finance and data protection is rooted in the development of Europe's capacity to formulate, monitor, and enforce regulation. Although their argument focuses on regulatory influence in general and not on extraterritoriality in particular, highly developed regulatory capacity does seem to be behind the EU's external regulatory influence. In the realm of finance, the spread of EU regulation has been facilitated by a group of regulators that has expertise and the ability to "punish" non-compliance by denying access to the EU financial market. In the area of data protection, the extensive reach of the EU Data Protection Directive has been buttressed by a coherent group of regulators that is capable of, with their expertise, making an "adequacy" determination of the privacy legislation of a non-EU country and, when necessary, imposing a ban on transfer of data to that country.

It should be noted, nonetheless, that the institutionalist argument of regulatory capacity does not deny the importance of market power. Rather, it is argued that market power must be combined with regulatory capacity to be effectively exerted.[11] By extension, it can be argued that the extraterritorial power of a state is substantiated by its market power *in combination with* its regulatory capacity.

Logic of Counter-Extraterritoriality

Since extraterritoriality represents a violation of the sovereign principle of territoriality and implies hierarchical relations, it can be reasonably expected to induce a backlash or what may be called "counter-extraterritoriality." In particular, extraterritoriality may lead to countermeasures when it generates negative impacts or externalities in a domestic system.

The logic of counter-extraterritoriality is the reverse of the logic of extraterritoriality; some sort of policy response may be called for to mitigate the negative effects that can arise from the beyond-the-border reach of laws and regulations. Such adverse effects may come in the way of "costs" on domestic entities (e.g. firms having to bear extra financial costs to comply with regulation).

More significantly, cross-border exercise of authority from one jurisdiction may have undermining effects on the integrity or operation of the domestic legal and regulatory regime in another. For example, the EU reacted sharply to the US Sarbanes-Oxley Act of 2002 because the legislation had multiple provisions with extraterritorial reach that challenged the European corporate governance regime as well as threatening to impose considerable costs on European firms that listed in the US (Bach and Newman 2007; Posner 2009).[12] Somewhat similarly, the extraterritorial clause of the EU Data Protection Directive became a cause of concern for the US not only because it could disrupt the operations of American enterprises that engaged in business with Europe but also because it would pressure the US to bear the cost of making internal adjustments (i.e. introducing European-style comprehensive privacy legislation) to meet the directive's "adequate data protection" requirement for the transfer of personal data to a third country.

Responses to Regulatory Extraterritoriality

What courses of action, then, can be taken against the extraterritorial assertion of foreign regulatory authorities? Borrowing from a study on policy diffusion by Simmons (2001), the argument can be made that, roughly speaking, states may attempt to deal with regulatory extraterritoriality through (1) positive reaction, (2) negative reaction, or (3) no reaction.

No Reaction

One possible response to extraterritoriality is simply to acquiesce to the unilateral claim from foreign authorities. While a pure example of "no reaction" is hard to find, "no action" may be an option for the receptive government when the extraterritorial act in question has little or negligible effect on domestic policy. For example, the Japanese government thus far has let European anti-competition authorities *directly* send questionnaires and "requests for information" to firms within the jurisdiction of Japan, although technically it can prohibit the giving of evidence or the production of documents in foreign proceedings. This is presumably because such extraterritorial law enforcement of the EU merely involves requests for information and does not demand changes in Japan's regulatory policy or regime.

Negative Reaction

By contrast, "negative reaction" entails aggressive response to claims of authority from another jurisdiction. Specifically, the receptive state may enact new legislation or invoke existing legislation to allow entities within the jurisdiction to continue the act prohibited by the foreign authority. Such legislation is not rare (Svantesson 2014). The receptive state may even resort to the enactment of "claw-back" legislation to recover the losses incurred by the extraterritorial regulation.

China's response to the EU ETS is a recent example of negative reaction. When the EU decided to include the aviation sector in its emissions trading scheme, the Chinese government "banned" all airlines in the country from joining the EU ETS, claiming that the plan could cost Chinese airlines 95 million euros in extra annual costs (BBC News 2012).

Arguably, negative reaction with blocking legislation has been a hallmark of Europe's response to the extraterritorial reach of US sanctions laws. More than once, the Europeans have acted against the unilateral imposition of US trade and investment regulations on companies operating outside US jurisdiction, even though the EU shares many of the foreign policy goals of the US (Ahearn 2007).

A prominent example of EU blocking legislation is Council Regulation (EC) 2271/96 of November 1996, which mandated corporations or individuals within the EU not to comply with any requirement or prohibition based on the Cuban Liberty and Democratic Solidarity Act of 1996 (also known as the Helms-Burton Act) or the Iran and Libya Sanctions Act of 1996 (also known as the D'Amato Act). However, this was not the first time US extraterritoriality provoked a backlash in Europe. When in 1982 the US extended outside its jurisdiction a ban on the sale of oil and gas equipment to the Soviet Union, European governments were outraged, and France went to the extent of ordering French companies to fulfill their contracts with the Soviets to supply equipment for a Siberia pipeline project (Hufbauer et al. 2007).

A caveat is that, given a risk of retaliation, an overtly defiant response to "dominant" powers' assertion of control is likely to be a privilege of relatively large countries.[13] If so, market size would matter in a country's strategy to counter extraterritoriality.

Positive Reaction

Between the two extremes of subordination and outright rejection is a range of "positive reaction." While negative reaction entails actions in the opposite direction, positive reaction involves actions by the receptive state in the same direction as that which the assertive state is pushing toward.

Emulation is a positive reaction in a narrow sense. In some cases, the receptive state takes over the policy preferred by foreign authorities under the threat of sanctions. In other cases, however, the receptive state embraces a unilaterally promoted policy for its anticipated benefit (Kahler and Lake 2009). The introduction of biometric passports in the EU is a case in point. Under the Enhanced Border Security and Visa Entry Reform Act of 2002, the US required the participant states of the Visa Waiver Program to implement biometric identifiers (e.g. digital facial images and fingerprints) in their passports (Hosein 2004). However, the US requirement accelerated, rather than forced, the adoption of Council Regulation (EC) 2252/2004 on standards for security features and biometrics in passports issued by EU member states. In all likelihood, the EU had little difficulty in adapting to the US policy because the Council had already resolved to strengthen the security of passports in 2000 (European Commission 2009a).

In a broader sense, positive reaction includes bargaining through which the receptive state seeks to manage problems, particularly to reduce adjustment costs associated with extraterritorial regulations. For example, when the Sarbanes-Oxley Act was passed in the US Congress, the EU sought to obtain exceptions from the newly imposed obligations for publicly listed corporations and certifying accountants. The US eventually made concessions as the EU threatened to retaliate by creating EU auditing legislation that would have the same extraterritorial effects as the US law.[14]

The EU–US Safe Harbor negotiations provide another example of "positive" reaction. When the EU adopted the Data Protection Directive in 1995, the US came up against the possibility of a data ban that might be imposed by the directive on a third country lacking an "adequate level of protection" (Swire and Litan 1998; Shaffer 2000). Therefore, the US proposed to the EU that American companies abiding by a set of privacy principles be exempted from the extraterritorial clause of the directive (Farrell 2003). The result was a scheme of mutual recognition that allowed the US to maintain a privacy regime that relied heavily on self-regulation (Bessette and Haufler 2001).

Conclusion

Extraterritoriality is a multi-faceted phenomenon. In some cases, extraterritorial jurisdiction is claimed on the basis of a nationality tie. In other cases, domestic law and regulation become extraterritorial in their reach as they are applied to entities engaging in activities across territories. In yet other cases, domestic law and regulation are applied extraterritorially to deal with negative effects arising from a foreign jurisdiction.

However, having a rationale of extraterritoriality is one thing, and exerting actual extraterritorial influence is another. To influence foreign or transactional conduct, regulators can leverage access to the domestic market or take advantage of the presence of an entity in the domestic market. It can be, therefore, argued that the effectiveness of extraterritorial regulation depends on the power derived from the domestic or internal market. Such market power, nonetheless, is exerted in combination with regulatory capacity.

It is important to note that extraterritorial regulation has distributional implications because it imposes the assertive state's preference on the receptive state and thereby forces the latter to bear the cost of adjusting policy and practice. Hence, the reaction of the receptive state depends on the nature and extent of the externalities or costs produced by the trans-border exertion of regulatory authority. When such a cost is politically or economically unacceptable, it is expected that the receptive state might react negatively and resist the extraterritorial claim of the assertive state. When the cost is not exorbitantly high but is still substantial, it is expected that the receptive state might react positively and attempt to reduce the adjustment cost through bargaining or negotiations. However, reaction to an extraterritorial regulatory claim is shaped by a political—rather than legal—process, in which involved actors seek to have their preferences reflected in the outcome.

Notes

1 It is worth noting that, by definition, extraterritoriality does not occur if the world consists of a single jurisdiction.

2 Traditionally, diplomats and conduct on an embassy's premises are subject to the laws of the home country and immune from the legal obligations of the host country.

3 EEA covers the 28 EU member states, plus Iceland, Liechtenstein, and Norway.

4 In this legal entanglement, the US Sherman Antitrust Act was applied to the allegedly monopolistic activities of the Aluminum Company of America (Alcoa) in Europe on the ground that such activities distorted the international market for aluminum ingot and harmed US producers and consumers (Putnam 2009).

5 Conversely, growing convergence in regulation across countries may result in a shift from extraterritoriality to a global system. See Sassen (2006, pp. 236–40).

6 It can be argued that extraterritoriality provides an alternative (particularly for dominant powers) to international cooperation, in which states mutually adjust their policies in accordance with consensually negotiated common rules (e.g. international agreements).

7 For example, the US Department of the Treasury could effectively pressure the Macao-based Banco Delta Asia, which was accused of laundering money for the North Korean government, by designating it a "primary money laundering concern" under the US Patriot Act and threatening to cut the bank off completely from the US financial system (Loeffler 2009).

8 Drezner (2007) argues, "For the current era of globalization, the economic great powers are the United States and the European Union. These are the only two entities that combine relatively large markets with relatively low vulnerability" (pp. 35–6).

9 The FCPA makes it "unlawful for a US person, and certain foreign issuers of securities" to bribe a foreign official, and foreign companies that list stocks on the US securities exchange market are "issuers" in the US (Darrough 2010).

10 Raustiala (2009) emphasizes that, historically, the practice of extraterritoriality developed in conjunction with the rise of the "regulatory state."

11 Drezner (2007) even argues that "regulatory capacities are of marginal importance without market size" (p. 227).

12 The Sarbanes-Oxley Act was a response to the Enron and other scandals involving US corporations, but it contained provisions that would directly affect non-US firms.

13 The receptive state can resort to a (quasi-)supranational institution, if available, without regard to the country size. For example, Antigua and Barbuda in 2003 lodged a complaint with the World Trade Organization (WTO) about the US prohibition on cross-border supply of internet gambling services (Scott 2005).

14 One of the exceptions concerned the requirement for audit committee independence. The Sarbanes-Oxley Act required, among other things, that a corporate board and an audit committee should be independent. However, German firms are required by their home country law to include representatives of employees in their auditing committee. This conflict of laws was resolved by the exception US securities authorities made concerning who could serve on an auditing committee (Posner 2009).

3 The EU Data Protection Directive

In October 1995, the European Union (EU) adopted Directive 95/46/EC on the protection of individuals with regard to the processing of personal data and on the free movement of such data (Data Protection Directive),[1] the cornerstone of the EU data protection regime. The directive was transposed into the national laws of EU member countries by October 1998.

While made in connection with the integration of the EU Internal Market, the Data Protection Directive has had far-reaching effects beyond the jurisdiction of the EU, because it has provisions on the transfer of personal data to countries that are not part of the EU (i.e. third countries). This so-called extraterritorial clause of the directive is an important legal background against which the EU and the United States (US) have had a series of talks over the transfer of personal data.

Currently, the Data Protection Directive is being replaced by the General Data Protection Regulation as part of a comprehensive reform of data protection rules in the EU. Similarly to the Data Protection Directive, the General Data Protection Regulation would have significant extraterritorial implications as it contains detailed provisions on the transfer of personal data to third countries.

The EU Data Protection Directive

The EU Data Protection Directive was formulated in the context of the creation of a European Single Market that had been completed at the end of 1992. It was expected that in the Single Market, not only goods, money, and people but also information, would flow "freely" among member countries. However, discrepancies in data protection could impede the free flow of personal information throughout the EU (Bennett and Raab 2006). For example, if an information practice permitted in one country was prohibited in another, information exchange between them would be hampered.

At the same time, differences in data protection laws and regulations could lead to uneven protection at the EU level (Newman 2008a). If some jurisdictions had weaker data protection safeguards than others, firms might relocate their data-processing operations in these "data havens" to evade strict data protection regulations of higher-standard countries. Such a situation would be detrimental to the European data protection regime as well as the rights of individuals whose data were processed in lower-standard countries. To ensure a constant level of protection of personal data across the EU, while allowing free flow of data in the Single Market, data protection legislation of the member states of the EU needed to be harmonized by an EU-level instrument.

Accordingly, the Data Protection Directive has the twin objectives of the protection of personal data in the jurisdiction of the EU *and* the free movement of personal data among EU countries. Under the directive, member countries are required to "protect the fundamental rights and freedoms of natural persons, and in particular their right to privacy with respect to the processing of personal data" (Article 1.1). Assuming that the equivalent level of data protection is ensured, member countries are then required not to restrict or prohibit the free flow of personal data between them for reasons connected with data protection (Article 1.2).

It is important to note that, in the Data Protection Directive, data protection is regarded as a right of individuals. The directive is not unique in this respect. In Europe, the right to privacy,[2] including data privacy, is generally considered as a fundamental human right. Indeed, the right to privacy is enshrined in Article 8 of the Charter of Fundamental Rights of the European Union,[3] which recognizes that "[e]veryone has the right to the protection of personal data concerning him or her."[4]

Under the Data Protection Directive, nonetheless, data protection is not merely a human rights issue but is explicitly linked to the operation of the European Single Market (Bennett and Raab 2006). In fact, the legal basis of the directive is Article 100a of the Treaty establishing the European Community, that is, "to ensure the establishment and functioning of the Internal Market." Technically speaking, therefore, the Data Protection Directive was adopted with regard to the Internal Market of the EU.

EU Data Protection Rules

In essence, the Data Protection Directive is designed to protect the data privacy right of individuals within the jurisdiction of the EU by regulating the use of personal data. The directive provides as follows:

- Personal data must be "(a) processed fairly and lawfully; (b) collected for specified, explicit and legitimate purposes and not further processed in a way incompatible with those purposes …; (c) adequate, relevant and not excessive in relation to the purposes for which they are collected and/or further processed;" and "(d) accurate and, where necessary, kept up to date" (Article 6);
- Special categories of data or sensitive data, defined as "personal data revealing racial or ethnic origin, political opinions, religious or

philosophical beliefs, trade-union membership" and "data concerning health or sex life" cannot be processed without permission (Article 8);

- Data subjects (i.e. individuals) are entitled to be informed about who collected the data relating to them, for what purpose the data are processed, and further information (Article 10);
- Data subjects are guaranteed to have access to the data relating to them "without constraint at reasonable intervals and without excessive delay or expense" as well as the right to rectify, erase, or block incomplete or inaccurate data (Article 12).

However, the scope of these obligations and rights can be restricted when such a restriction constitutes a necessary measure to safeguard national security, defense, public security, or "the protection of the data subject or of the rights and freedoms of others" (Article 13).

Extraterritorial Clause

The Data Protection Directive includes not only provisions on the processing of personal data within the jurisdiction of the EU but also provisions on the transfer of personal data to third countries. Specifically, Article 25.1 provides as follows:

> The Member States shall provide that the transfer to a third country of personal data which are undergoing processing or are intended for processing after transfer may take place only if, without prejudice to compliance with the national provisions adopted pursuant to the other provisions of this Directive, the third country in question ensures an adequate level of protection.

In other words, Article 25.1 provides that transfer of personal data to a third country can only take place when the third country in question ensures an "adequate level of protection" of personal data. The adequacy of the level of protection, in turn, is to be assessed "in the light of all the circumstances surrounding a data transfer operation or set of data transfer operations," and, in particular, consideration is given to "the nature of the data, the purpose and duration of the proposed processing operation or operations, the country of origin and country of final destination, the rules of law, both general and sectoral, in force in the third country in question and the professional rules and security measures which are complied with in that country" (Article 25.2).

But who decides the adequacy? The European Commission, the executive body of the EU, does. If the European Commission finds that a third country does not ensure an adequate level of protection, "Member States shall take the measures necessary to prevent any transfer of data of the same type to the third country in question" (Article 25.4). In other words, member countries are mandated—rather than permitted—to ban the transfer of data to a third country that the European Commission considers inadequate.

However, an inadequacy finding does not necessary mean a definitive data ban. The European Commission is required to "enter into negotiations with a view to remedying the situation" resulting from the inadequacy finding (Article 25.5). Upon conclusion of the negotiations, the European Commission may find that a third country ensures an adequate level of protection by reason of the international commitments it has entered into (Article 25.6).

In addition, data can be transferred to a third country deemed inadequate by way of "derogations" (Article 26). Such data transfers are possible when (a) there is unambiguous consent of the data subject, (b) the transfer is necessary for the performance of a contract, (c) the transfer is necessary or legally required on important public interest grounds, or (d) the transfer is necessary in order to protect the vital interests of the data subject. Data can also be transferred through contractual clauses.[5]

The rationale behind the extraterritorial provision of the Data Protection Directive is that, in a world where data flow across borders, data privacy regulation must reach beyond the originating jurisdiction if it is to meaningfully protect the right of a data subject. Suppose an EU citizen's personal data are transferred to a third country and misused there. Then that individual's right to data privacy would be infringed. Such infringement of rights, in turn, would suggest a failure of data protection and thus undermine the effectiveness of the EU data protection regime. In other words, conduct in foreign jurisdictions can undermine the integrity of the domestic regulatory regime of the EU as well as the right of individuals in the EU, and the extrajurisdictional reach of the Data Protection Directive is expected to be instrumental to mitigating such negative effects.

"Protectors of Privacy"

The Data Protection Directive requires each member country to have "one or more public authorities [who] are responsible for monitoring the application within its territory of the provisions adopted by the Member States pursuant to this Directive" (Article 28.1).[6] Each authority should be endowed with investigative powers and effective powers of intervention, including the power "of ordering the blocking, erasure or destruction of data" and the power "of imposing a temporary or definitive ban on processing" (Article 28.3).

In accordance with Article 29 of the directive, representatives of national supervisory authorities form an independent advisory body called the Working Party on the Protection of Individuals with regard to the Processing of Personal Data or "Article 29 Working Party." Essentially, the Article 29 Working Party was established to supervise the implementation of the Data Protection Directive at the EU level. As a group of data protection experts, the Working Party examines any question covering the application of the national measures adopted under the directive (Article 30.1) and makes recommendations on all matters relating to the protection of persons with regard to the processing of personal data in the EU (Article 30.3).

Importantly, the Working Party gives the European Commission an opinion on the level of protection in the Community and in third countries (Article 30.1). Thus, the European Commission in actuality makes an "adequacy decision" on the basis of an expert opinion of the Article 29 Working Party. In this sense, the European "protectors of privacy" (Newman 2008b) could be in a position to effectively influence the adequacy decision of the European Commission.

General Data Protection Regulation

On January 25, 2012, the European Commission proposed a comprehensive reform of data protection rules in the EU "to increase users' control of their data and to cut costs for businesses" (European Commission 2012b). The centerpiece of this initiative was the proposal for two legislative instruments: one was a regulation that set out a general EU framework for data protection, and the other was a directive on protecting personal data processed for law enforcement purposes.

After four years of work, on April 8, 2016, the Council of the EU adopted Regulation (EU) 2016/679 on the protection of natural persons with regard to the processing of personal data and on the free movement of such data[7] (General Data Protection Regulation) and Directive (EU) 2016/680 on the protection of natural persons with regard to the processing of personal data for the purposes of the prevention, investigation, detection, or prosecution of criminal offences, or the execution of criminal penalties, and on the free movement of such data.[8] On April 14, 2016, the European Parliament also adopted the Regulation and the Directive. The Regulation is scheduled to apply from May 25, 2018, and the Directive is scheduled to be implemented by May 6, 2018.

In essence, the General Data Protection Regulation was enacted to update and modernize the 1995 Data Protection Directive, which the regulation is going to replace. Like the Data Protection Directive, the General Data Protection Regulation has the twin objectives of the protection of data and free movement of such data within the EU. However, the two instruments are different in how they are implemented. A directive sets out a goal that all EU countries must achieve, but individual countries have latitude in devising their own laws on how to reach these goals. A regulation, on the other hand, is a binding legislative act and must be applied in its entirety across the EU.[9] Thus, while the Data Protection Directive was implemented differently across member countries, the General Data Protection Regulation is designed to provide a single set of rules on data protection across the EU.

For businesses, the simplified regulatory environment is expected to reduce administrative costs. Under the regulation, firms will have to comply with a single pan-European law, instead of up to 28 different national laws. On a related note, firms will have to deal with a single national data protection authority. This means that a firm with subsidiaries in several member countries will only have to deal with the data protection authority in the EU country where it has its main establishment. At the same time, the General Data Protection Regulation imposes new obligations on data controllers (i.e. companies). For example, companies must notify the national supervisory authority of serious data breaches (Article 33). Compliance with the obligations under the regulation will be monitored by the competent supervisory authority, which is granted the sanctioning power to impose administrative fines of up to 20 million Euro or 4 percent of the total worldwide annual turnover of a company (Article 83).

For individuals, the benefits of the General Data Protection Regulation would lie in the consistent application of a set of data protection rules, including strengthened rights of data subjects. Specifically, the regulation sets out the following:

- the need for the individual's clear consent to the lawful processing of personal data (Article 6);
- easier access by the individual to his or her personal data (Article 15);
- the "right to be forgotten"[10] (Article 17);
- the "right of data portability" from one service provider to another (Article 20); and
- the right to object, including to the use of personal data for the purposes of "profiling" (Article 21).

Third Country Transfers under the General Data Protection Regulation

As for third country transfers, the General Data Protection Regulation provides as follows:

> A transfer of personal data to a third country or an international organisation may take place where the Commission has decided that the third country, a territory or one or more specified sectors within that third country, or the international organisation in question ensures an adequate level of protection.
>
> (Article 45)

In other words, transfers of personal data to third countries or international organizations may be based on an adequacy decision by the European Commission. A number of elements, including relevant legislation "concerning public security, defence, national security and criminal law and the access of public authorities to personal data," are to be taken into account in assessing the adequacy of the level of protection.

Where the Commission has not taken an adequacy decision on a territory or sector, transfer of personal data may still take place if there are appropriate safeguards (Article 46). Such safeguards are mainly provided by the following:

- a legally binding and enforceable instrument between public authorities or bodies;
- binding corporate rules[11];
- standard data protection clauses; and
- contractual clauses.

In short, the General Data Protection Regulation contains detailed provisions on the transfer of personal data to third countries or international organizations, requiring that such transfer can take place only if the conditions laid down in the regulation are met. The logic behind the extraterritorial provisions is the same as that of the Data Protection Directive. If personal data are transferred to a third country or an international organization and misused there, the efficacy of the EU data protection regime as well as the rights of the individual whose data were inappropriately processed would be undermined. To safeguard the integrity of the EU data protection regime and the rights of data subjects, the EU regulation on data privacy needs to be extended beyond the jurisdiction of the EU.

Conclusion

The Data Protection Directive is said to be "the most influential international policy instrument to date" (Bennett and Raab 2006, p. 93) in the field of data privacy. In particular, Article 25 (and 26) of the Data Protection Directive has had major implications for international businesses that rely on transborder flows of personal data, including credit-granting and financial institutions, hotel and airline reservations systems, the direct-marketing sector, life and property insurance, the pharmaceutical industry, and any online company that markets its products and services worldwide (Bennett and Raab 2006). To receive personal data from the EU, these businesses need to comply with the EU rules on data transfer.

The extraterritorial clause also became a cause of concern for governments of third countries. If a third country was deemed "inadequate" by EU standards, companies and other organizations in that country would have trouble with importing data from the jurisdiction of the EU. The extraterritorial impact of the directive, indeed, is the main force behind the development of a series of arrangements between the EU and the US.

Similarly to the Data Protection Directive, the General Data Protection Regulation has provisions on the transfer of data to third countries. Their extraterritorial implications would be significant in the digital age, in which data might be collected in Berlin, processed in Boston, stored in Bangalore, and accessed from Beijing. By setting standards for data transfer, the General Data Protection Regulation could be a source of EU influence over data protection regulation in other jurisdictions as well as a cause of friction between the EU and other jurisdictions.

Notes

1 Directive 95/46/EC of the European Parliament and of the Council of 24 October 1995 on the protection of individuals with regard to the processing of personal data and on the free movement of such data.

2 Article 8 of the European Convention on Human Rights recognizes that "[e]veryone has the right to respect for his private and family life, his home and his correspondence." The convention was developed by the Council of Europe and came into force in 1953.

3 The Charter of Fundamental Rights of the European Union was proclaimed in 2000 and became legally binding on the EU with the entry into force of the Treaty of Lisbon in December 2009.

4 Article 16 of the Treaty on the Functioning of the European Union (TFEU) also declares that "[e]veryone has the right to the protection of personal data concerning them."

5 In June 2001 the European Commission adopted a decision that set standard contractual clauses to ensure adequate safeguards for personal data transferred from the EU to third countries (Bennett and Raab 2006).

6 Supervisory authorities had been established in EU countries since the 1970s. According to Newman (2000a, b), the adoption of the Data Protection Directive was the culmination of decade-long efforts by a transnational coalition of European data protection authorities, which framed the issue of EU-level data protection as a prerequisite to further market and administrative integration in Europe.

7 Regulation (EU) 2016/679 of the European Parliament and of the Council of 27 April 2016 on the protection of natural persons with regard to the processing of personal data and on the free movement of such data, and repealing Directive 95/46/EC.

8 Directive (EU) 2016/680 of the European Parliament and of the Council of 27 April 2016 on the protection of natural persons with regard to the processing of personal data by competent authorities for the purposes of the prevention, investigation, detection or prosecution of criminal offences or the execution of criminal penalties, and on the free movement of such data, and repealing Council Framework Decision 2008/977/JHA.

9 European Commission, "Regulations, Directives and other acts," https://europa.eu/european-union/law/legal-acts_en, accessed August 26, 2016.

10 The right to be forgotten is the right of data subjects to have their data deleted if the data are no longer necessary or there are no legitimate grounds for the processing of the data.

11 Binding corporate rules cover transfers within a group of companies that engage in a joint economic activity (particularly, a multinational corporation) and expressly confer rights on data subjects with regard to the processing of their personal data (Article 47).

4 From Safe Harbor to Privacy Shield

Data privacy and protection issues have long been sticking points in economic and security relations between the European Union (EU) and the United States (US) (Weiss and Archick 2016). Precisely because they are tied with the flows of data—along with flows of goods, services, and people—the transatlantic difference in approaches to data privacy has raised tensions between the EU and the US.

To defuse such tensions, the EU and the US have had talks over the transfer and use of data that contain personal information. The first round of EU–US data talks was held in the late 1990s to avoid what could have been the first trade conflict of the information age, resulting in the 2000 Safe Harbor arrangement (later called the "Safe Harbor framework") under which personal data could legally be transferred from EU territory to the US for commercial purposes. Recently, the EU and the US have agreed to replace the Safe Harbor with a new framework, the Privacy Shield. The purpose of the Privacy Shield framework, nevertheless, is the same as that of the Safe Harbor arrangement: allowing US companies and other organizations to send and receive personal data across the Atlantic, while complying with the requirements of EU data protection laws.

The Extraterritorial Reach of the EU Data Protection Directive

The EU–US negotiations that led to the Safe Harbor arrangement were precipitated by the adoption in October 1995 of the EU Data Protection Directive, the cornerstone of the EU data protection regime. While establishing a regulatory framework for the protection of personal data within the EU, the Data Protection Directive had "clear external consequences" (Farrell 2003, p. 285) or "extra-jurisdictional effect" (Shaffer 2000, p. 55), because it set conditions for the transfer of personal data to third countries (i.e. non-EU countries). Specifically, the directive provides that transfer of personal data to a third country can take place only when the third country in question ensures an "adequate level of protection" of personal data (Article 25.1). "The adequacy of the level of protection afforded by a third country," in turn, "shall be assessed in the light of all the circumstances surrounding a data transfer operation," including the "rules of law … in force in the third country in question" (Article 25.2).

This extraterritorial provision of the EU directive had particularly serious implications for the US, because the US has taken a quite different approach to data privacy from that of the EU and thus was unlikely to meet the adequacy requirement of the directive (Swire and Litan 1998).

The transatlantic difference in approach to privacy is of no minor significance. In the EU, a comprehensive regime has developed through legislation to protect personal data processed in both the public and private sectors, with the Data Protection Directive being the lynchpin of this regime. Furthermore, the enforcement of data protection laws is overseen at the national and EU levels by regulatory authorities (i.e. data protection authorities) that have expertise and statutory sanctioning power (Newman 2008b; Farrell 2003).

In the US, by contrast, a relatively limited regime has developed in the absence of overarching privacy law. While information practices of the US federal government and its agencies are regulated by the Privacy Act of 1974, handling of personal data held by private entities is regulated by a patchwork of rules that deal with specific sectors, such as financing and telecommunications.[1] Many sectors are not covered by specific laws and instead rely on self-regulation by industry or firms. Added to that, the US lacks a regulatory body, akin to European data protection authorities, to monitor compliance and enforcement of privacy laws (Shaffer 2000; Charlesworth 2000; Farrell 2003).

It has been argued that such differences are deeply rooted in different philosophies of social regulation. In Europe, privacy is considered to be a fundamental right (as enshrined in Article 8 of the European Convention on Human Rights and Articles 7 and 8 of the Charter of Fundamental Rights of the EU) and a matter of social protection. This means that an individual's right to data privacy is to be protected by law and government regulation. In the US, on the other hand, rights are generally seen as rights against the government. Accordingly, the US approach is to protect the privacy of consumers and users (rather than citizens or data subjects) largely through market pressures and self-regulation of firms or industry,[2] rather than legislation—which in essence is an exercise of state power in regulating the processing of personal data—and government oversight (Shaffer 2000; Farrell 2003; Kobrin 2004; Bennett and Raab 2006).

US Response

To allow for continued flow of data, the US Department of Commerce and the European Commission, the executive body of the EU, entered into negotiations over the transfer of data from the EU to the US. However, it was not until the first half of 1998 that real discussion began. To the Europeans' dismay, the US government was slow to realize that the European

Commission was not going to accept the US privacy regime as adequate and that, consequently, some action needed to be taken to remedy the situation (Farrell 2003; Kobrin 2004; Heisenberg 2005).

It seemed to the US that the EU was trying to impose its privacy rules in an extraterritorial fashion (Swire and Litan 1998). However, the US could not flatly ignore the European privacy rules, foremost because the US and EU had close economic ties. The US and the EU, indeed, were each other's largest trading partners (Shaffer 2000).[3] Since head-on confrontation with the EU could lead to costly disruption of transatlantic trade, it was virtually impossible for the US to repudiate the third-country transfer rules of the Data Protection Directive as an extraterritorial application of EU law.

The EU–US Safe Harbor Negotiations

From the outset of the negotiations,[4] there was an understanding between the European Commission and the US government that data should continue to flow across the Atlantic.[5] In an extreme case, if the directive was implemented to the letter, the flows of personal data from the EU to the US could be interrupted, but neither the EU nor the US wanted such interruption. The problem, thus, was not *whether* but *how* personal data should be transferred from EU territory to the US. How could companies in the US—which was unlikely to be deemed to provide "adequate protection" by EU standards—import personal data from the territory of the EU without fear of being punished by the data protection authorities of EU member countries for violating the Data Protection Directive?[6]

The EU was concerned that the US approach could not guarantee a sufficient level of protection for data originating in the EU (Bessette and Haufler 2001). In fact, the Working Party on the Protection of Individuals with regard to the Processing of Personal Data (Article 29 Working Party) took the view that the "patchwork of narrowly-focussed sectoral laws and voluntary self-regulation" could not "be relied upon to provide adequate protection in all cases for personal data transferred from the European Union" (Article 29 Working Party 1999, p. 2). EU negotiators, therefore, insisted on the need for formal legislation in the US (Farrell 2003).

However, the US steadfastly argued that personal information transferred to the US could be adequately protected by industry self-regulation (Bessette and Haufler 2001). Indeed, self-regulation was the Clinton administration's preferred means of solving privacy problems (Farrell 2003). In a policy paper titled the "Framework for Global Electronic Commerce," released in July 1997, the administration advocated that the private sector should lead the emerging digital economy without government intervention. With regard to privacy, the administration made it clear that "private efforts of industry working in cooperation with consumer groups" were "preferable to government regulation" (Clinton and Gore 1997).

It should be noted that the EU and the US each had a preferred solution that might have had "negative potential repercussions" for the other (Farrell 2003, p. 291). If the US were found to meet the adequacy requirement of the directive, despite the lack of a comprehensive law to protect personal data processing in the private sector, the credibility of the directive would be impaired (Bennett and Raab 2006). In other words, if the negotiation outcome were to reflect the US preference for self-regulation, the EU data privacy regime based on a legislative approach would be undermined. Alternatively, if the outcome were to reflect the EU's preference for formal legislation, the US government's efforts to promote self-regulation would be undercut. Hence, concern about the impact of an EU–US arrangement on the US data privacy regime overshadowed the entire process of negotiations (Kobrin 2004).

The logjam in the negotiations was eventually cleared by the conceptual breakthrough of a "safe harbor" whereby US organizations were to be sheltered from sanctions by EU authorities. David Aaron, the Undersecretary for Trade in the US Department of Commerce, who had work experience on Wall Street, is credited with bringing the idea into the negotiations (Farrell 2003). Under the scheme that Aaron proposed, US companies that self-declared to adhere to a set of data privacy principles ("Safe Harbor Principles") would be allowed to receive personal data from the EU as they would be deemed to provide "adequate protection."

The crucial point is that adequacy would be judged on an organization-by-organization basis rather than on a country-by-country basis (Kobrin 2004; Heisenberg 2005). While Article 25 of the Data Protection Directive provides that data can only be transferred if the third *country* in question ensures an adequate level of protection, the Safe Harbor scheme allows data to be transferred if the *organization* (i.e. *company*) in question ensures an adequate level of protection.

The European Commission officials were cautious of the US proposal at first, partly because making a self-regulatory exception in the Data Protection Directive for the US could undermine the directive's efficacy. However, as there were few alternatives that might prevent a trade conflict with the US, the European Commission agreed to think about the concept of the Safe Harbor (Heisenberg 2005). The negotiations then came to concentrate on the content of the Safe Harbor Principles and the associated enforcement mechanisms.

In the second part of 1998, the Department of Commerce wrote the outlines of a Safe Harbor proposal and received feedback from the European Commission on various elements of the document (Heisenberg 2005). The Commerce Department proposed a first set of Safe Harbor Principles in November 1998. The Principles were further developed in consultation with the European officials as well as US industry. As such, the European Commission had opportunities in the drafting process to help dictate the terms of the transfer and use of personal data by US companies (Farrell 2003).

On March 14, 2000, the US Department of Commerce and the European Commission reached an arrangement on a safe harbor system with the understanding that the arrangement would come into effect on November 1, 2000. US Secretary of Commerce William M. Daley hailed the Safe Harbor arrangement as a "data privacy success" that "comes none too soon to support the growth of the almost 2 trillion dollar US–EU trade and investment relationship," particularly in the rapidly growing electronic-commerce sectors (US Department of Commerce 2000). On the EU side, Internal Market Commissioner Frits Bolkestein said, "the 'safe harbor' will help us to tap the huge potential of the information revolution by providing legal certainty for operators and privacy safeguards for consumers" (European Commission 2000a).

The Safe Harbor Arrangement

The Safe Harbor arrangement is neither a treaty nor an international agreement but basically consists of two unilateral actions: the issuance of the Harbor Principles and frequently asked questions (FAQs) by the US Department of Commerce, and the adoption of an "adequacy decision"[7] on the Safe Harbor Principles by the European Commission (Kobrin 2004).

The Department of Commerce published the final version of the Safe Harbor Principles on July 21, 2000. The Principles were intended to serve as authoritative guidelines to US companies and other organizations that receive personal data from the EU, supplemented by the FAQs that provide guidance for implementation.[8] The Principles are the following.

- Notice: An organization must inform individuals about the purposes for which it collects and uses information about them, how to contact the organization with any inquiries or complaints, the types of third parties to which it discloses the information, and the choices and means the organization offers individuals for limiting its use and disclosure.
- Choice: An organization must offer individuals the opportunity to choose (i.e. opt out) whether their personal information is to be disclosed to a third party or to be used for a purpose that is incompatible with the purpose(s) for which it was originally collected or subsequently authorized by the individual. For "sensitive information,"[9] individuals must be given affirmative or explicit (i.e. opt-in) choice.
- Onward transfer: To disclose information to a third party, organizations must apply the Notice and Choice Principles. Where an organization wishes to transfer information to a third party, that party provides at least the same level of privacy protection as is required by the relevant Principles.
- Security: Organizations must take reasonable precautions to protect information from loss, misuse and unauthorized access, disclosure, alteration, and destruction.
- Data integrity: Personal information must be relevant for the purposes for which it is to be used. An organization may not process personal

information in a way that is incompatible with the purposes for which it has been collected. An organization should ensure that data is reliable for its intended use, accurate, complete, and current.

- Access: Individuals must have access to personal information about them that an organization holds and be able to correct, amend, or delete that information where it is inaccurate.
- Enforcement: Effective privacy protection must include mechanisms for assuring compliance with the Principles, recourse for individuals to whom the data relate affected by non-compliance with the Principles, and consequences for the organization when the Principles are not followed.

For its part, the European Commission, on July 26, 2000, adopted a decision (the "Safe Harbor decision") recognizing that the Safe Harbor Principles, implemented in accordance with the guidance provided by the FAQs, "are considered to ensure an adequate protection for personal data" transferred from the EU to the US (European Commission 2000b).[10]

While the "safe harbor" is an innovative idea for privacy regulation, the Safe Harbor Principles consist of rather common and familiar information practices. In fact, the Safe Harbor Principles are largely consistent with the basic principles of the Organisation for Economic Co-operation and Development (OECD) Privacy Guidelines, which both the US and the EU have approved. For example, Safe Harbor's "data integrity" principle is consistent with the "data quality" principle of the OECD Guidelines, which requires that "personal data should be relevant to the purposes for which they are to be used, and, to the extent necessary for those purposes, should be accurate, complete and kept up-to-date." Furthermore, Safe Harbor's "data integrity" principle is also consistent with the Data Protection Directive's principles relating to "data quality," which provide that personal data must be, among other things, "adequate, relevant and not excessive in relation to the purposes for which they are collected and/or further processed" (Article 6).

Unlike the OECD Guidelines, however, the Safe Harbor Principles do not include the "use limitation" principle (i.e. personal data should not be disclosed, made available, or otherwise used for purposes other than those specified at the time of collection).[11] In this regard, the Safe Harbor Principles are also different from the EU Data Protection Directive that provides that data must "not be further processed in a way incompatible with those purposes" (Article 6). It may be argued that the Safe Harbor Principles, in a sense, are more business-friendly, allowing firms to use personal data more flexibly than the OECD Privacy Guidelines or the EU Data Protection Directive.

Enforcement of the Safe Harbor

The functioning of the Safe Harbor primarily relied on commitments and self-certification of firms that participated in the scheme. Under the Safe Harbor, firms and other organizations voluntarily adhered to the Safe

Harbor Principles, but they bound themselves publicly to the Principles in order to sign up to the "Safe Harbor" list of the Department of Commerce and benefit from the Safe Harbor arrangement. Compliance with the Principles might be checked in the first instance by private-sector bodies such as BBBOnline and TRUSTe through trustmark "privacy seal" programs.[12] Such a self-regulatory scheme was the first layer of the enforcement of the Safe Harbor.

The second layer of the Safe Harbor enforcement mechanism involved a federal government agency, namely, the US Federal Trade Commission (FTC). This made the entire scheme a hybrid of government enforcement and self-regulation (Farrell 2003). As a "backstop" to self-regulation, any public misrepresentation or non-compliance (i.e. breaking of commitment under the Safe Harbor) would be subject to legal sanctions by the FTC under Section 5 of the Federal Trade Commission Act, which prohibits "unfair or deceptive acts or practices in or affecting commerce."

According to Farrell (2003), this hybrid mechanism was a policy innovation that resulted from a dialogue between EU and US officials. Heisenberg (2005), however, argues that the enforcement mechanism bore a strong imprint of US industry. In fact, the Safe Harbor arrangement largely overlapped with the policy proposal of the Online Privacy Alliance (OPA), a consortium of around 50 companies organized to protect consumer privacy on the internet.[13] The OPA's policy toward online consumer data privacy was articulated in its November 1998 white paper, which concluded the following:

> Self-regulatory programs such as OPA's, which are designed to operate in the context of the United States' layered approach of self-regulation backed by government enforcement, should be recognized as effective by the EU in its effort to protect privacy while promoting the uninterrupted flow of global commerce.
>
> (OPA 1998)

In other words, the enforcement mechanism of the Safe Harbor arrangement largely reflected the preferences of US industry (and its champion, the US government) to the extent that it allowed for continued self-regulation and the "layered" approach" favored by the OPA (Bessette and Haufler 2001).[14]

"Snowden Revelation" and EU–US Negotiations

For 15 years, the EU–US Safe Harbor arrangement served as a basis for transatlantic transfer of personal data for commercial purposes. While (supposedly) protecting the privacy rights of Europe's more than 500 million citizens, the arrangement allowed for uninterrupted flows of data from companies in the EU to the companies in the US that had signed up to the Safe Harbor program. About 4,500 companies, including not only internet and technology companies but also non-tech companies, benefited from the

Safe Harbor as they could "freely" send and receive data, including personal information, across the Atlantic (Weiss and Archick 2016).

However, the Safe Harbor arrangement was controversial in Europe from the start, and serious questions were raised about the adequacy of data protection under the scheme (Kobrin 2004). In an Opinion of May 2000, the Article 29 Working Party called for further improvements of the Safe Harbor Principles, notably the principles of access, choice, and onward transfer (Article 29 Working Party 2000). The European Parliament in its resolution of July 2000 also called for changes to be made to the Safe Harbor Principles so that they would include an individual right of appeal to an independent public body and an obligation on participating firms to compensate for damages (European Parliament 2000).

A turning point for the Safe Harbor framework—and other EU–US data agreements—was the revelation of mass surveillance by US authorities. From early June 2013, it was revealed in media that the US National Security Agency (NSA) had collected information, such as search histories and the content of emails, file transfers, and chats, directly from the servers of Internet companies, including Google, Facebook, Apple, Microsoft, and Yahoo, in a secret program code-named PRISM (Greenwald and MacAskill 2013; Gellman and Poltras 2013). The revelation—primarily based on documents provided by the former NSA contractor Edward Snowden—"sparked an international debate on the consequences of such large-scale electronic surveillance for citizens' privacy" (Article 29 Working Party 2014, p. 4).

The revelation of the US surveillance program raised deep concerns over the protection of personal data transferred to the US under the Safe Harbor scheme, because all companies involved in the PRISM program—which granted US authorities access to data stored and processed in the US—appear to have been Safe Harbor certified. In other words, the Safe Harbor framework seemed to have acted as a conduit through which US intelligence authorities were given access to personal data that were initially processed in the EU (European Commission 2013c).

Under the Safe Harbor arrangement, adherence to the Safe Harbor Principles may be limited "*to the extent necessary* to meet national security, public interest, or law enforcement requirements" (italics added). The question, then, was whether the large-scale collection and processing of personal information under US surveillance programs was necessary and proportionate to meet the interests of national security (European Commission 2013e).

On November 27, 2013, the European Commission issued a communication titled "Rebuilding Trust in EU–US Data Flows" (European Commission 2013b). In the communication, the Commission suggested that the following steps should be taken to restore trust in data transfers for the benefit of the digital economy, security both in the EU and in the US, and the broader transatlantic relationship:

1 a swift adoption of the EU's data protection reform;
2 making Safe Harbor safer;
3 strengthening data protection safeguards in law enforcement cooperation;
4 addressing European concerns in the ongoing US reform process; and
5 promoting privacy standards internationally.

With regard to "Making Safe Harbor safer," the Commission made 13 recommendations to improve the functioning of the scheme, which focused on the issues of (a) transparency, that is, increased transparency of certified companies' privacy policies; (b) redress, that is, enhanced availability and affordability of dispute resolution mechanisms; (c) enforcement, that is, more effective supervision and monitoring by the US authorities of the compliance of certified companies with the Safe Harbor Principles; and (d) access by US authorities, that is, ensuring that the use of the national security exception provided in the Safe Harbor would be limited to what was strictly necessary and proportionate.

Against this background, discussions began in January 2014 between the European Commission and the US Department of Commerce for a new framework for transatlantic data transfer. In the view of the Commission, "strengthening" the Safe Harbor scheme was preferable to suspending or revoking the Safe Harbor decision as the "revocation would adversely affect the interests of member companies in the EU and in the U.S." (European Commission 2013c, p. 7). However, critics of the Safe Harbor arrangement, notably the European Parliament, called for immediate suspension of the Safe Harbor.[15] In a resolution of March 12, 2014, the European Parliament called on the European Commission to present measures that would immediately suspend the Commission's adequacy decision on the Safe Harbor as the Parliament considered that "under the current circumstances the Safe Harbour Principles do not provide adequate protection for EU citizens" (European Parliament 2014, 38). In the view of the European Parliament, large-scale access by US intelligence agencies to EU personal data transferred under the Safe Harbor scheme did not meet the criteria for "national security" derogation (European Parliament 2014, 37).

The Schrems Case and the EU–US Negotiations

A ruling by the Court of Justice of the EU (CJEU, commonly referred to as the European Court of Justice or the ECJ) then sealed the fate of the Safe Harbor framework. On October 6, 2015, the CJEU issued a decision, which, among other things, found that the Europeans Commission's adequacy decision on the Safe Harbor arrangement was invalid.

The CJEU investigated the validity of the Safe Harbor adequacy decision in connection to a complaint lodged by Maximillian Schrems, an Austrian law student and a Facebook user, with the Data Protection Commissioner of Ireland.[16] Schrems claimed that, in light of the "Snowden revelation," the law and practice of the US did not offer sufficient protection against surveillance by the public authorities of the data transferred to the US (e.g. data provided to Facebook by its European subscribers and then transferred to the servers in the US via its Irish subsidiary). The CJEU observed that national security, public interest, and law enforcement requirements of the US prevailed over the Safe Harbor scheme, so that US undertakings were bound to disregard, without limitation, the protective rules laid down by the Safe Harbor scheme where they conflicted with such requirements. As such, the CJEU found that the Safe Harbor scheme enabled interference by US public authorities with the fundamental rights of persons and did not provide a sufficient level of data protection as required by EU law (CJEU 2015).[17]

Following the CJEU's ruling, the European Commission and the US government stepped up the ongoing negotiations, because the invalidation meant that the Safe Harbor arrangement could no longer serve as a legal basis for the transfers of personal data from the EU to the US.[18] Negotiators were driven by a sense of urgency. For one thing, businesses, particularly technology companies, were concerned about uncertainty over transatlantic data flows and called on the European Commission and the US government to conclude a new Safe Harbor agreement "as soon as possible."[19] For another, the Article 29 Working Party, in a statement of October 16, 2015, on the consequences of the ECJ's judgment, announced that "[i]f by the end of January 2016, no appropriate solution is found with the U.S. authorities … EU data protection authorities are committed to take all necessary and appropriate action, including coordinated enforcement actions" (Article 29 Working Party 2015, paragraph 5).

On February 2, 2016, the European Commission and the Department of Commerce announced an agreement, in principle, on the replacement of the Safe Harbor with the Privacy Shield to allow companies to continue to transfer personal data from the EU to the US (European Commission 2016). US Secretary of Commerce Penny Pritzker praised the "historic agreement" as (US Department of Commerce 2016). Věra Jourová, European Commissioner for Justice and Consumers, on the other hand, said the following:

> The new EU–US Privacy Shield will protect the fundamental rights of Europeans when their personal data is transferred to U.S. companies … . In the context of the negotiations for this agreement, the US has assured that it does not conduct mass or indiscriminate surveillance of Europeans.
>
> (European Commission 2016a)

The Privacy Shield Framework

Like its predecessor, the Privacy Shield consists of unilateral actions by the US and the EU. On the US side, the Privacy Shield package includes a set of privacy rules ("Privacy Shield Principles"), commitments of the Department of Commerce, a letter from the FTC,[20] a letter from the Department of Transportation,[21] a letter prepared by the Office of the Director of National Intelligence (ODNI), a letter from the Department of State, and a letter prepared by the Department of Justice.

The Privacy Shield Principles basically are an extended version of the Safe Harbor Principles. They include—in line with the European Commission's call for greater transparency—a substantially longer list of notice requirements; tightened conditions for onward transfers; and detailed provisions on recourse, enforcement, and liability.

- Notice: An organization must inform individuals about its participation in the Privacy Shield, the types of personal data collected, the purposes for which it collects and uses personal information about them, how to contact the organization with inquiries or complaints, the type of third parties to which it discloses information and the purposes for which it does so, the right of individuals to access their personal data, the choices and means the organization offers individuals for limiting the use and disclosure of information, the independent dispute resolution body designated to address complaints, the requirement to disclose personal information in response to lawful requests by public authorities, and its liability in cases of onward transfers to third parties.
- Choice: An organization must offer individuals the opportunity to choose (i.e. opt out) whether their personal information is to be disclosed to a third party or to be used for a purpose that is materially different from the purpose for which it was originally collected or subsequently authorized by the individuals. For sensitive information, organizations must obtain affirmative express consent (i.e. opt in) from individuals.
- Accountability for onward transfer: To transfer personal information to a third party, organizations must comply with the Notice and Choice Principles. Organizations must also enter into a contract with the third party that provides that such data may only be processed for limited and specified purposes and that the recipient will provide the same level of protection as the Principles.
- Security: Organizations must take reasonable and appropriate measures to protect information from loss, misuse and unauthorized access, disclosure, alteration, and destruction.
- Data integrity and purpose limitation: Personal information must be limited to the information that is relevant for the purposes of processing. An organization may not process personal information in a way that is incompatible with the purposes for which it has been collected. An organization must ensure that personal data is reliable for its intended use, accurate, complete, and current.
- Access: Individuals must have access to personal information about them that an organization holds and be able to correct, amend, or

delete that information where it is inaccurate, or has been processed in violation of the Principles.

- Recourse, enforcement, and liability: Effective privacy protection must include robust mechanisms for assuring compliance with the Principles, recourse for individuals who are affected by non-compliance with the Principles, and consequences for the organization when the Principles are not followed. Organizations and their selected independent recourse mechanisms will respond promptly to inquiries and requests by the Department for information relating to the Privacy Shield. A Privacy Shield organization has responsibility for the processing of personal information it receives under the Privacy Shield and subsequent transfers to a third party. When an organization becomes subject to an FTC or court order based on noncompliance, the organization shall make public any relevant Privacy Shield-related sections of any compliance or assessment report submitted to the FTC.

As for supervision, the Department of Commerce has committed to monitoring how companies comply with their commitments to adhere to the Principles. If a Privacy Shield company fails to comply, the Department of Commerce will remove the company from the Privacy Shield List the department keeps. Like the Safe Harbor, companies' commitments are binding and enforceable by the FTC.

Redress mechanisms are also strengthened along the line of the European Commission's recommendations. EU individuals now have several possibilities to obtain redress: they can inquire or complain directly to the company, use free-of-charge alternative dispute resolution, or take their complaints to their "home" data protection authority.

In addition, the US government agreed to establish an annual review mechanism, which would allow the EU officials to monitor the functioning of the Privacy Shield, including the limitations and safeguards relating to national security access. The US also agreed to establish a new Privacy Shield Ombudsperson for submission of inquiries regarding US intelligence practice within the State Department.

Perhaps most significantly, the US government, through the letters from the Office of the Director of National Intelligence and the Department of Justice, provided the EU for the first time with written assurance that access to data by public authorities for national security and law enforcement would be subject to limitations, safeguards, and oversight mechanisms. The letter prepared by the Office of the Director of National Intelligence states the following:

> In short, the IC [Intelligence Community] does not engage in indiscriminate surveillance of anyone, including *ordinary European citizens*. Signals intelligence collection only takes place when duly authorized and in a manner that strictly complies with these limitations; only

> after consideration of the availability of alternative sources, including from diplomatic and public sources; and in a manner that prioritizes appropriate and feasible alternatives [*italics* added].[22]

Furthermore, the letter prepared by the Department of Justice states the following:

> All law enforcement and regulatory activities in the United States must conform to applicable law, including the U.S. Constitution, statutes, rules, and regulations. Such activities must also comply with applicable policies … The legal framework described above limits the ability of U.S. law enforcement and regulatory agencies to acquire information from corporations in the United States – whether the information concerns U.S. persons or *citizens of foreign countries* … [*italics* added].[23]

Behind this statement was Presidential Policy Directive 28 (PPD-28) issued in January 2014 by then president Barack Obama concerning signals intelligence activities. PPD-28 sets out a series of principles and requirements that apply to all US signals intelligence activities and to all people, *regardless of nationality or location*. In particular, it sets certain requirements for procedures to address the collection, retention, and dissemination of information. Importantly, it also directs that protections afforded to the personal information of US persons be extended to personal information of non-US persons.

At the same time, PPD-28 does not rule out bulk collection of data by intelligence authorities. Indeed, the letter from the Office of the Director of National Intelligence points out that PPD-28 "provides that signals intelligence collected in bulk can only be used for six specific purposes … ."[24] In other words, while "assuring" that the US intelligence agencies will not engage in indiscriminate surveillance, the letter suggests that bulk collection of data may take place under specific circumstances. It may be argued, therefore, that the "Privacy Shield presents a confusing picture with regard to its coverage of mass surveillance or the bulk collection of data by US intelligence or national security agencies" (Kuner 2016, p. 21).

The European Commission's Adequacy Decision

On the EU side, the European Commission on February 29, 2016, published a draft "adequacy decision" that recognized that "the United States ensures an adequate level of protection for personal data transferred from the Union to organisations in the United States under the EU–U.S. Privacy Shield" (European Commission 2016e).

In response, the Article 29 Working Party issued an opinion on April 13, 2016. In the opinion, the Working Party, while welcoming "significant improvements," expressed strong concerns on both the commercial aspects and the access by public authorities to data transferred under the Privacy Shield. In particular, the Working Party claimed that the representations of the ODNI did not provide sufficient details of the measures to exclude massive and indiscriminate collection of personal data originating from the EU (Article 29 Working Party 2016). For its part, the European Parliament adopted a resolution on May 26 on transatlantic data flows and called on the European Commission "to implement fully the recommendations expressed by the Article 29 Working Party in its Opinion" (European Parliament 2016b).

On July 12, the European Commission adopted the Privacy Shield and notified the "adequacy decision" to the member states (European Commission 2016e). The adequacy decision entered into force immediately. According to Commissioner Jourová, "[t]he new framework will restore the trust of consumers when their data is transferred across the Atlantic" (European Commission 2016d).

Conclusion

The Safe Harbor arrangement emerged from efforts by the EU and the US to allow continued flows of data across the Atlantic. According to its cover letter, the "safe harbor is a landmark accord for e-commerce" that "bridges the differences between EU and U.S. approaches to privacy protection and will ensure that data flows between the U.S. and the EU are not interrupted."[25] Since the EU and the US were (and still are) each other's largest trade partners, and data flows were part of trade, both parties arguably stood to benefit from the arrangement.

From the viewpoint of the US, the Safe Harbor arrangement was made to manage the extraterritorial effects of the EU directive on US firms as well as the US privacy regime. When the EU adopted the Data Protection Directive in 1995, the US came up against the possibility of a data ban that might be imposed by the directive on a third country lacking an "adequate level of protection." Thus, the US negotiated with the EU and proposed that US companies abiding by a set of privacy principles be exempted from the extraterritorial clause of the directive. The result was a scheme of mutual recognition that allowed the US to maintain a privacy regime that relied heavily on industry self-regulation (Bessette and Haufler 2001).

It is important to note that the Safe Harbor arrangement was made as a way to allow US companies and other organizations to receive data from the EU *without* requiring the US to introduce formal legislation (i.e. a comprehensive data privacy law) (Farrell 2003). Nor was the Safe Harbor meant to set a precedent for future change in the US privacy regime. Rather, the Safe Harbor allowed the US government to claim that, while establishing a predictable framework for data transfer, its basic policy stance of protecting privacy through self-regulation was unchanged.

From the standpoint of the EU, on the other hand, the Safe Harbor deal was struck to protect the integrity of the European data protection regime as well as the rights of EU data subjects. By slightly changing the interpretation of Article 25 of the Data Protection Directive, the Safe Harbor accord allowed the EU to maintain the adequacy requirement for data transfer; personal data could be transferred to an *organization* in the US only if the *organization* in question ensured an "adequate" level of protection.

After the CJEU's decision had struck down the Safe Harbor scheme, EU and US negotiators created a successor framework, the Privacy Shield, for the continued flows of data. Similarly to the Safe Harbor, the Privacy Shield does not require the US to enact new legislation. It should be recalled that the US responded to the EU's concern about the undermining effects of US surveillance with a "written assurance" rather than an enactment or amendment of laws regarding intelligence activities. It remains to be seen whether this non-legalistic approach of the US is effective in ensuring "adequate protection" of data transferred from the EU.

It is worth noting that, through the Safe Harbor arrangement and the Privacy Shield framework, the EU has exerted a *certain* level of influence over the information practices of US private organizations (i.e. firms) that import personal data from the EU. In essence, both the Safe Harbor and the Privacy Shield set conditions under which personal data originating in the EU can be transferred to and subsequently used in the US. It has been revealed, however, that the Safe Harbor failed to provide sufficient protection of EU citizens' personal data against disproportionate use by US intelligence agencies.

Will the Privacy Shield have an impact on the information practices of US public authorities? On the face of it, the Privacy Shield framework does limit US public authorities' use of the personal data sent from the EU. Despite the written assurance from the US government, however, it is not yet certain whether the Privacy Shield will actually provide effective safeguards against mass surveillance or bulk collection of data.

At the same time, while no EU institutions have jurisdiction over US public authorities, EU authorities have leverage to influence the behavior of US companies that might receive data originating in the EU. Through their influence over private entities that might provide data to US authorities, the regulatory authorities of the EU might indirectly have *some* impact on the information gathering and processing by US intelligence and law enforcement authorities.

Notes

1 Examples include the Fair Credit Reporting Act of 1971, the Cable Communication Policy Act of 1984, the Electronic Communications Privacy Act of 1986, and the Videotape Privacy Protection Act of 1988.

2 In theory, firms can improve their reputations and hence market position vis-à-vis competitors through good privacy protection practices (Shaffer 2000).

3 Furthermore, the EU was the site of most US foreign investment (Shaffer 2000). As a matter of practice, the affiliates of US firms (particularly US-based

multinational firms) that operated in the EU depended on transatlantic flow of personal data for their routine business activities.

4 The EU delayed enforcing the Data Protection Directive's provisions on third-country transfers while negotiations took place (Shaffer 2000).

5 The Data Protection Directive provides that the European Commission should "enter into negotiations with a view to remedying the situation resulting from the finding" that a third country does not ensure an adequate level of protection (Article 25.5).

6 Technically, data transfer to countries where protection is not deemed adequate could still take place by way of "derogations" (Article 26). For example, such transfer might be authorized if the data subject has given his or her consent unambiguously to the proposed transfer or if safeguards are provided through "contractual clauses." However, these alternative mechanisms tended to be cumbersome and thus were not very practical solutions.

7 Commission Decision of 26 July 2000 pursuant to Directive 95/46/EC of the European Parliament and of the Council on the adequacy of the protection provided by the safe harbour privacy principles and related frequently asked questions issued by the US Department of Commerce, 2000/520/EC.

8 https://new.export.gov/community/pages/65-safe-harbor-privacy-principles, accessed August 8, 2016.

9 Sensitive information is defined as "personal information specifying medical or health conditions, racial or ethnic origin, political opinions, religious or philosophical beliefs, trade union membership or information specifying the sex life of the individual." This definition is consistent with the definition in the Data Protection Directive.

10 Under Article 25 of the Data Protection Directive, the European Commission may decide that a non-EU country ensures an "adequate level of protection." See chapter 3.

11 Another difference from the OECD Privacy Guidelines is the inclusion of "choice." Under Safe Harbor, organizations can collect personal information for one purpose and use it for another, unless individuals *opt out*.

12 Alternatively, firms may sign up to cooperate directly with EU data protection authorities.

13 The OPA was one of a number of voluntary efforts to protect privacy that were directed at warding off potential regulatory action by government (Bessette and Haufler 2001).

14 Not surprisingly, consumer groups reacted critically to the Safe Harbor proposal, arguing that the proposal lacks an effective means of enforcement or redress for privacy violations. In particular, the Transatlantic Consumer Dialogue (TACD), a coalition of EU and US consumer groups, urged the European Commission and the Ministers of the European Council to reject the Safe Harbor proposal (Bessette and Haufler 2001).

15 Earlier on, the European Parliament in a resolution of July 4, 2013, called on the European Commission "to conduct a full review of the Safe Harbour Agreement in the light of the recent revelations" (European Parliament 2013a).

16 *Maximillian Schrems v Data Protection Commissioner* case (C-362-14).

17 Furthermore, the CJEU observed that the European Commission had merely examined the Safe Harbor scheme, although the Commission had been required to find that the US ensured, by reason of its domestic law or its international commitments, an adequate level of protection of privacy rights (CJEU 2015).

18 Businesses could pursue data transfers on the basis of Standard Contractual Clauses and Binding Corporate Rules, but the European Commission took the view that a new general arrangement was the best way in an age of ever-increasing commercial data transfers across the Atlantic (European Commission 2015a).

19 DIGITALEUROPE's reaction to the CJEU Judgement in the case Maximillian Schrems vs Data Protection Commissioner (Case C-362/14), October 6, 2015. DIGITALEUROPE represents the digital technology industry in Europe, and its members include Apple, Google, and Microsoft.
20 It describes the FTC's enforcement of the Privacy Shield.
21 It describes the Department of Transportation's enforcement of the Privacy Shield.
22 Letter from General Counsel Robert Litt, Office of the Director of National Intelligence (European Commission 2016e, Annex VI).
23 Letter from Deputy Assistant Attorney General and Counselor for International Affairs Bruce Swartz, US Department of Justice (European Commission 2016e, Annex VII).
24 *Ibid.*
25 Cover Letter. July 21, 2000. Robert S. LaRussa, Acting Under Secretary for International Trade Administration. Available at www.export.gov/safeharbor/eu/eg_main_018494.asp. Accessed September 2, 2009.

5 The PNR Dispute

Since the 1990s, the European Union (EU) and the United States (US) have had a series of talks over the transfer of personal data across the Atlantic. As detailed in the previous chapter, the EU and the US in 2000 established a framework for the commercial transfer and use of personal data in an effort to promote an information-based economy in general and electronic commerce in particular. The terrorist attacks of September 11, 2001, then profoundly changed the landscape of transatlantic politics around data transfer. After the attacks, transfer and use of personal data came to be discussed in the context of security and law enforcement cooperation rather than in the context of the rise of the digital economy. The EU–US disputes over air passenger data that led to the passenger name record (PNR) agreements signify this change, highlighting the ever more difficult problem of striking a balance between data privacy and public security.

The Extraterritorial Reach of US Counterterrorism Regulation

The PNR dispute began with the US decision to use information on air passengers for counterterrorism purposes. In the wake of the September 11 terrorist attacks, the US Bureau of Customs and Border Protection (CBP) within the Department of Homeland Security (DHS) started requiring air carriers operating passenger flights to or from the US to electronically submit PNR data stored in their computer reservation/departure control systems (US Department of Homeland Security n.d.). This requirement was backed up by substantial threat of sanctions. If airlines refused to submit PNR data, they would be subject to fines of thousands of dollars per passenger and could even lose their landing rights (Heisenberg 2005).

A PNR is the travel record for a person, containing the passenger's name, date of birth, address, telephone number, method of payment, choice of meal, and other information (Hailbronner et al. 2008; Bennett 2005). While a PNR is collected and used for commercial purposes (e.g. booking an air ticket), such data are considered useful to conduct efficient and effective advance risk assessment of passengers (US Department of Homeland

Security n.d.). In other words, PNR data are thought to be helpful to profile passengers and identify terrorists, thereby mitigating negative effects that may arise from transactions with foreign jurisdictions. Indeed, the requirement to transfer PNR data can be seen as an expression of the US government's desire to "exercise extraterritorial control over the movement of goods and people" flying into US territory (Rees 2006, p. 97).

The regulation that mandated the submission of PNR data was based on a US domestic law, namely the Aviation and Transportation Security Act of 2001, which was hurriedly passed only a few weeks after the terrorist attacks. However, the measure had considerable beyond-the-border effects as it was applied to *all* international passenger flights landing on US soil. Flights departing from Europe were no exception. If anything, radical young Muslims in Western Europe, who could travel to the US without a visa, were seen with grave concern by US law enforcement authorities (Argomaniz 2009).

The EU's Response

The US government's program to use PNR data for counterterrorism sparked a vehement reaction in the EU "because it undermined the extensive European regulation in the field of data protection" (Pawlak 2009a, p. 565). As noted, PNRs contain personal data of air passengers, and transfer of PNR data to the CBP was conceivably inconsistent with the EU data protection rules enumerated in the Data Protection Directive.

To begin with, it was against the purpose limitation principle to use data originally collected for air travel for other purposes (i.e. public security). Article 6 of the Data Protection Directive stipulates that data should be "collected for specified, explicit and legitimate purposes and not further processed in a way incompatible with those purposes." Furthermore, the amount of data involved was arguably so large that it was questionable whether they were to be considered as "adequate, relevant and not excessive" in relation to the purposes for which they were collected and/or further processed, as articulated in Article 6 of the Data Protection Directive, as well as Article 8 of the European Convention on Human Rights (Article 29 Data Protection Working Party 2002). Equally significant, the transfer of PNR data to the US government agency was likely inconsistent with Article 25—the so-called extraterritorial provision—of the Data Protection Directive, because the privacy law applicable to US federal authorities protected only the data of US citizens, leaving EU citizens outside the scope of legal protection.

Thus, European airlines were caught between EU privacy laws and US security regulations. If they did not observe the legal obligations in the US, they would be subject to sanctions by the US government. The stakes were high. Airlines carried at least 10–11 million people a year from Europe to the US (Article 29 Working Party 2003). Conversely, if air carriers complied with the US requirement, they would violate the extraterritorial provision of the EU Data Protection Directive and face sanctions by European data protection authorities (Hailbronner et. al. 2008).

The EU–US PNR Negotiations (1)

Technically, the EU could rely on the Data Protection Directive to curtail the extraterritorial exercise of US authority. The directive provides that transfer of personal data to a third country may be halted if the country in question does not ensure an "adequate level of protection" (Article 25). Alternatively, it was not totally impossible for the EU to temporarily acquiesce to the US demand just as other trading partners of the US had done under the extreme circumstances in the aftermath of the terrorist attacks. It may even be argued that if the EU had been overwhelmed by the hegemonic influence of the US, it would have taken the course of "no action." Since European airlines had already begun sending the PNR data stored in their databases to the CBP, inaction by the EU would mean the continued supply to the US of a major tool to fight terrorism—that is, information exchange (Balzacq 2008).[1]

In reality, the European Commission entered into negotiations with the Department of Homeland Security to establish a legal framework for the transfer of PNR data from EU territory and the subsequent use of data in the US. According to European Commissioner Frits Bolkestein, the EU was "solidly behind the US in the need to combat terrorism," but he found that the "at best legally fragile" situation should "not be allowed to continue" (Bolkestein 2003). Importantly, while the EU and the US disagreed on important details, the "right" of the US government to use PNR data in its fight against terrorism was not in question (Heisenberg 2005). Thus, the EU–US negotiations centered not on *whether* PNR data should be transferred and used but on *how* such data should be made available to US authorities.[2] In other words, the issue in dispute was not the legitimacy of using PNR data for counterterrorism purposes but the rules and conditions surrounding its implementation (Newman 2011).

After prolonged negotiations the EU and the US reached an agreement on the processing and transfer of PNR data in December 2003 (US Department of Homeland Security 2003). As part of the deal, the Department of Homeland Security gave "undertakings" that explained the manner in which the CBP would handle the PNR data obtained from European airlines. The European Commission subsequently made a decision that recognized the adequate protection of PNR data transferred to the CBP, and the Council of the EU[3] decided on the conclusion of the agreement. The EU–US PNR agreement (PNR I) was formally concluded in May 2004. The European Commission claimed that "a balanced solution" had been negotiated (European Commission 2004c).

However, European data protection authorities were not convinced that satisfactory progress had been made in the EU–US negotiations. Acting collectively as the Article 29 Working Party, the "protectors of privacy" demanded that respect for fundamental rights and freedom of the individual, including the right to privacy and data protection, should be ensured particularly by limiting the scope of the data to be transferred, their retention period, and the way in which they would be used (Article 29 Working Party 2004a, b).

The European Parliament was also concerned with the privacy implications of the PNR agreement. Unlike the European Commission, the Parliament gave the most attention to the problems of data protection (Pawlak 2009a). In March 2004, the Parliament adopted a resolution that called on the European Commission to withdraw the draft decision on the adequacy of the CBP's handling of PNR data originating in the EU. The Council, nonetheless, signed the agreement as the Parliament's resolution was nonbinding. In a dramatic move, the Parliament in July 2004 filed a case at the European Court of Justice (ECJ). Following the argument presented by data protection authorities, the Parliament claimed that, in addition to having chosen an incorrect legal basis, the agreement was in violation of the fundamental principles of the Data Protection Directive as well as the fundamental right and the principle of proportionality (joined cases C-317/04 and C-318/04).

In May 2006, the ECJ ruled against the PNR agreement because it did not have an appropriate legal basis. Sidestepping the question of data privacy, the Court found that the Commission's adequacy decision could not have been based on the "first-pillar" directive on data protection, or the Council's decision to approve the conclusion of the PNR agreement on a Community law dealing with the internal market, because PNR transfer was a "third-pillar" issue of public security.[4]

As a consequence, the PNR agreement of 2004 was annulled, and the Council of the EU, assisted by the European Commission, launched negotiations with the Department of Homeland Security under the auspices of the "third pillar." In spite of the changes on the EU side, the EU–US negotiations continued to center on the rules and conditions—rather than the necessity—of PNR transfer and use as the Council was generally in favor of using PNR data in the fight against terrorism (Newman 2011).[5]

The EU and US negotiators managed to hammer out an interim agreement (PNR II) in October 2006 and made a longer-term agreement (PNR III) in July 2007 (European Parliament 2010). In wrapping up the renegotiations, Secretary of Homeland Security Michael Chertoff sent a letter ("US letter to EU") to assure the EU of the safeguarding of PNR data. In a reply ("EU letter to US"), Council President Luis Amado confirmed that the EU would deem that the Department of Homeland Security had ensured an adequate level of protection.

The EU–US PNR Agreements of 2004 and 2007

With the immediate objective of rescuing airlines from a legal limbo, the PNR agreement in essence aimed at finding a solution to the "legal compatibility problems" (Pawlak 2009a, p. 565). From the viewpoint of the EU, "legal" transfer and use of PNR data was to be consistent with the European data privacy principles.

While the EU was unable to get the US to change its data privacy regime, it did get an agreement that would bring the US authorities' use of PNR data originating in the EU closer to the European principles, particularly the proportionality principle (i.e. processing of personal data must be "adequate, relevant and not excessive in relation to its purpose"). Specifically, the PNR agreements of 2004 and 2007 provided as follows:

- the Department of Homeland Security would use the transferred data for the purposes of preventing, detecting, investigating, and prosecuting terrorism and other serious transnational crimes instead of a wider range of criminal offences that it had originally requested;
- the Department of Homeland Security would receive fewer elements of data (34 elements under the 2004 agreement and 19 elements under the 2007 agreement) than it had initially proposed (50–60 elements);
- "sensitive data"[6] as defined in the Data Protection Directive (i.e. personal data and information revealing racial or ethnic origin, political opinions, religious or philosophical beliefs, trade union membership, or data concerning the health or sex life of the individual) would not be allowed to be used;[7]
- the data would be retained for a shorter period of time (3.5 years under the 2004 agreement and 15 years—five years in an "active" database and ten years in a "dormant" database—under the 2007 agreement) than it had originally sought (50 years);
- the Department of Homeland Security would share PNR data originating in the EU only with other domestic government authorities with law enforcement, public security, or counterterrorism functions (under the 2007 agreement);
- PNR data originating in the EU would be only exchanged with other government authorities in third countries after consideration of the recipient's intended use(s) and ability to protect the information (under the 2007 agreement); and
- the rights of EU data subjects would be protected under US laws[8] (Privacy International 2004; Newman 2008b; Pawlak 2009a).

It is important to note that, by guaranteeing to safeguard PNR data originating in the EU, the US in effect agreed to restrict the use of personal data that might be of great value to counterterrorism. This negotiation outcome is highly remarkable, given that "there was a perception in some parts of the US government that as security concerns became more important … personal information privacy could legitimately be traded off for greater public security" (Heisenberg 2005, p. 140).

According to Newman (2008, 2010, 2011), the US made concessions to the EU in such a way as to have European data protection principles reflected in the agreements, because European data protection authorities—which had statutory power to impose sanctions against businesses that engaged in "illegal" data transfers—provided EU negotiators with leverage to persuade the US government to comply with EU data protection rules[9] (Newman 2011). However, the influence of data protection authorities should not be overemphasized. The ECJ's decision of May 2006 placed the PNR issue under the "third pillar" (public security) and outside the "first pillar" (internal market) competence of data protection authorities. As such, data protection authorities played a relatively minor role in the negotiations leading to the 2007 PNR agreement. Rather, it seems that the data protection authorities' most valuable means of influence was their close working relationship with the European Parliament, which was involved in the PNR matter both formally and informally (Pawlak 2009a).

The EU–US PNR Negotiation (2)

While made in response to the external pressure from the US, the PNR agreement was to be deeply affected by the EU's internal changes. The European Parliament, which used to be sidelined on the "third pillar" issues, obtained the right to consent in most international agreements, including the PNR agreement, with the entry into force of the Lisbon Treaty in December 2009.

In May 2010, the European Parliament adopted a resolution that postponed its vote on the 2007 PNR agreement mainly due to data protection concerns. Accordingly, the European Commission and the US government in December 2010 began renegotiations and in November 2011 agreed on a revised arrangement on the transfer and use of PNR data (European Commission 2011a, c; European Parliament 2012a).

The European Parliament, of course, was not monolithic, and there was fervent debate. Some members supported the agreement because of the value of PNR data in the investigation of terrorist attacks and the capture of perpetrators. Others raised objections against the deal, echoing criticism from the Article 29 Working Party (2002, 2003, 2004) and the European Data Protection Supervisor (EDPS). In the words of rapporteur Sophie in t'Veld, "the European Parliament cannot credibly endorse an agreement that is not in line with EU privacy and data protection laws and principles" and that "creates a precedent that should not be underestimated given the growing number of countries requiring the transfer of PNR data" (European Parliament 2012b).

Nevertheless, the Parliament's opposition to the renewed PNR deal weakened for two reasons. First, there was a need for an agreement that would provide European airlines with a common EU legal basis for transferring PNR data. Without such basis, European airlines might have divergent responses to the US requirement. Second, there was concern that rejection of the agreement could result in the removal of EU countries from the US Visa Waiver Program. The European Parliament thus gave consent to the revised PNR agreement in April 2012, much to the distress of privacy advocates (European Parliament 2012c).

The EU–US PNR Agreement of 2012

The 2012 PNR agreement (PNR IV) differs from the 2007 agreement in having US "undertakings" formally incorporated into the main text. This means that the "undertakings" are no longer unilateral commitments but legally binding obligations of the US government. Hence, the legal certainty of the implementation of the agreement was expected to be enhanced.

In terms of the handling of data, nonetheless, the 2012 agreement at first glance may look more or less the same as its predecessors. The 2012 agreement provides the following:

- The Department of Homeland Security is allowed to collect, use, and process PNR data for the purposes of preventing, detecting, investigating, and prosecuting (a) terrorist offences and related crimes and (b) other crimes that are punishable by a sentence of imprisonment of three years or more and that are transnational in nature;
- 19 types of data are transferred;
- Sensitive data, as defined by the Data Protection Directive, are filtered and masked out from PNR data by automated systems;[10]
- Data are retained in an "active" database for up to five years and then transferred to a "dormant" database for a period of up to ten years;
- The Department of Homeland Security may share PNR data with domestic government authorities only for the purposes of preventing, detecting, investigating, and prosecuting terrorist offences and related crimes, and other crimes that are punishable by a sentence of imprisonment of three years or more and that are transnational in nature;
- The US may transfer PNR data to competent government authorities of third countries only under terms consistent with the agreement and only upon ascertaining that the recipient's intended use is consistent with those terms; and
- The US and the EU will jointly review the implementation of the agreement.

Compared with the 2007 agreement, however, the 2012 agreement provides for relatively enhanced protection of data subjects' (i.e. individuals') rights:

- In accordance with the provisions of the US Freedom of Information Act, any individual regardless of nationality, country of origin, or place of residence is entitled to request his or her PNR from the Department of Homeland Security;

- Any individual regardless of nationality, country of origin, or place of residence may seek the correction or rectification, including the possibility of erasure or blocking, of his or her PNR by the Department of Homeland Security;
- Any individual regardless of nationality, country of origin, or place of residence whose personal data and personal information have been processed and used in a manner inconsistent with the agreement may seek effective administrative and judicial redress in accordance with US law.

Another important difference between the 2012 and 2007 agreements is the method of PNR transmission of each. The PNR agreement of 2007 provides that, while PNR data will be eventually sent ("pushed") by airlines, US authorities will access the PNR data from air carriers' reservation systems located within EU member states until there is a satisfactory system in place to "push" data. The PNR agreement of 2012, on the other hand, recognizes the "push" method as, in principle, the only mode of transferring PNR data (European Commission 2011b).[11] Specifically, the 2012 agreement provides that "carriers shall be required to transfer PNR data to DHS using the 'push' method" (Article 15).

It should be noted that there is more to the choice between different data transfer methods than mere technical specifications. With a "pull" system, the CBP can decide the timing and frequency of data extraction and, theoretically, have broad access to data held in airlines' computer systems. It is then not surprising that US authorities clearly preferred to directly access ("pull") PNR data and allegedly were "doing all they [could] to ensure that they retain[ed] the ability to access the databases of airlines whenever and as often as they like[d]" (House of Lords 2007, points 125 and 129).[12] In fact, Homeland Security Secretary Chertoff stated the following in the "US letter to EU" that was attached to the 2007 PNR agreement:

> Given our recent negotiations, you understand that DHS is prepared to move as expeditiously as possible to a 'push' system of transmitting PNR from airlines operating flights between the EU and the U.S. to DHS … . The transition to a 'push' system, however, does not confer on airlines any discretion to decide when, how or what data to push. That decision is conferred on DHS by U.S. law.

With a "push" system, data transfer operations will be carried out *within the jurisdiction of the EU*, allowing European authorities to ensure that only information on relevant flights (i.e. flights bound to the US) be sent to the CBP and that sensitive data be filtered *within EU territory*.[13] Therefore, the Article 29 Working Party (2004b) insisted that airlines should replace the "pull" method of transferring data with the "push" method so that the US government would only be given the data it actually needed.

The European Parliament, the ally of data protection authorities, took a leading part in bringing about a change between the 2007 and 2012 agreements, particularly in the provisions on data transfer methods. The replacement of the "pull" with the "push" system, indeed, was one of the requests the European Parliament made in its resolution of May 5, 2010, which expressed "its determination to fight terrorism and organised and transnational crime, and, at the same time, its firm belief in the need to protect civil liberties and fundamental rights, while ensuring the utmost respect for privacy, informational self-determination and data protection" (European Parliament 2010). With the newly acquired veto power—the rejection of the Terrorist Financing Tracking Program (TFTP) agreement had set a precedent (Monar 2010)—the post-Lisbon European Parliament was in a strong position to pressure the European Commission, and by extension the US government, to ensure that a new agreement would meet the minimum privacy safeguard requirements listed in its resolution, which stated the following:

a PNR data may only be used for law enforcement and security purposes in cases of serious organized and transnational crime or terrorism of a cross-border nature;
b the use of PNR data for law enforcement and security purposes must be in line with European data protection standards, in particular regarding purpose limitation, proportionality, legal redress, limitation of the amount of data to be collected and of the length of storage periods;
c in no circumstances may PNR data be used for data mining or profiling; no "no-fly" decision or decision to investigate or prosecute may ever be taken based on the sole results of such automated searches or browsing of databases; use of data must be limited to specific crimes or threats, on a case-by-case basis;
d in the case of the transfer of PNR data of EU citizens to third countries, the terms of such transfers shall be laid down in a binding international treaty, providing legal certainty and equal treatment for EU citizens and companies;
e the onward transfer of data by the recipient country to third countries shall be in line with EU standards on data protection, to be established by a specific adequacy finding; this will apply equally to any possible onward transfer of data by the recipient country to third countries; and
f PNR data may only be provided on the basis of the "push" method.

(European Parliament 2010)

As noted earlier, the Parliament's exercise of power was constrained by internal and external considerations. Nevertheless, its presence was hefty enough to make US Attorney General Eric Holder tell the Parliament, "[w]e share your concern about privacy protection and civil liberties" (European Parliament 2011).

The Impact of the NSA Scandal

The latest PNR agreement (PNR IV) entered into force in July 2012 for a period of seven years. However, the agreement might be revised or renewed earlier than 2019 in light of recent developments in Europe and across the Atlantic.

First, the revelations since June 2013 of large-scale surveillance activities in Europe by the US National Security Agency (NSA) are likely to affect the information-sharing agreements between the EU and the US, including the PNR agreement. In fact, on July 4, 2013, the European Parliament adopted a resolution that expressed serious concern over PRISM and other such programs that "entail a serious violation of the fundamental right of EU citizens and residents to privacy and data protection" and suggested the possible suspension of the PNR and TFTP agreements with the US (European Parliament 2013a, points 1 and 4).

While the Parliament's resolution was largely symbolic and the PNR agreement notwithstanding remains in force (Archick 2016), the NSA scandal has reinforced EU demands for stronger levels of data protection in the US as well as for non-discriminatory treatment of EU data subjects with regard to the means of redress available in the US (Cîrlig 2016). To restore trust in the transatlantic relationship, a future PNR agreement would have to take these concerns into account.

The EU PNR System

Second, the prospective introduction of the EU's own PNR system in accordance with the 2016 PNR Directive might have a material effect on the EU–US PNR deal. Article 20 of the 2012 PNR agreement provides as follows:

> Given that the establishment of an EU PNR system could have a material effect on the Parties' obligations under this Agreement, if and when an EU PNR system is adopted, the Parties shall consult to determine whether this Agreement would need to be adjusted accordingly to ensure full reciprocity. Such consultations shall in particular examine whether any future EU PNR system would apply less stringent data protection standards than those provided for in this Agreement, and whether, therefore, this Agreement should be amended.

Presumably, this rather ambiguous "reciprocity" provision was inserted to address the problem of "reciprocity deficit," that is, one-sided transfer of PNR data from the EU to the US. As early as 2003, the European Commission stated as follows:

> any possible information exchange with the US authorities should be based on the principle of reciprocity in the transfer of data between the EU and the US, whilst at the same time considering the possibility for the collection and controlled transfer of PNR-data through a central European entity.
>
> (European Commission 2003d, p. 9)

The EU PNR Directive was proposed by the European Commission in February 2011. However, it failed to gain the support of the European Parliament, which was concerned with the data protection aspect of the proposal. Nevertheless, the EU PNR scheme continued to be discussed amid the perceived threats to the EU's internal security and came back under the spotlight after the January 2015 terrorist attack in Paris. The EU PNR Directive was formally approved by the European Parliament on April 14, 2016, and by the Council of the EU on April 21, 2016, respectively. The directive will oblige air carriers to provide member states' authorities with the PNR data for "extra-EU flights" (i.e. flights entering or departing from the EU). It will also allow member states to collect PNR data concerning selected "intra-EU flights" (i.e. flights from an EU country to one or more other EU countries), provided that they notify the European Commission (European Parliament 2016a, b; Council of the EU 2016c).

While it will take two years for the directive to enter into force, the establishment of the EU PNR systems may necessitate adjustment of the EU–US PNR agreement to ensure "full reciprocity," that is, exchange—rather than one-sided transfer—of PNR data between the EU and the US. A crucial question is whether such adjustment leads to changes in the data protection standards provided in the agreement.

The Umbrella Agreement

The third development that might affect the EU–US PNR agreement is the conclusion of the EU-US data protection "Umbrella Agreement" (also known as the "Data Privacy and Protection Agreement"). In essence, the Umbrella Agreement is intended to provide an overarching data protection framework for transatlantic data exchanges for law enforcement purposes. Nonetheless, it is relevant to specific agreements that provide a legal basis for actual transfers of data (e.g. the EU–US PNR agreement) in the sense that it creates comprehensive data protection rules for future agreements in the field of EU-US law enforcement cooperation (European Commission 2016g; Archick 2016; Cîrlig 2016).

The EU and the US officially began negotiations on the Umbrella Agreement on March 29, 2011, following the calls from the European Parliament and the Council.[14] After the revelation of the NSA's surveillance program, the negotiation of the Umbrella Agreement became part of efforts to restore trust in transatlantic data flows.[15] The agreement was initialed on

September 8, 2015. The Council of the EU provisionally signed the agreement on June 2, 2016. The European Parliament gave its consent for the conclusion of the agreement on December 1, 2016, and the next day, the Council of the EU adopted a decision authorizing the EU to conclude the agreement (European Commission 2016g; Council of the EU 2016b).

The Umbrella Agreement covers all personal data exchanged between police and criminal justice authorities of the EU member states and the US federal authorities for the purpose of prevention, investigation, detection, and prosecution of criminal offences, including terrorism. The agreement provides for general rules concerning purpose limitations, onward transfer, retention periods, right to access and rectification, and information in case of data security breaches (European Commission 2016g).

Perhaps most importantly, the Umbrella Agreement provides for equal rights of access to remedies in the US for EU citizens with regard to their personal data. To fulfill the condition for the agreement to be signed, the US Congress passed the Judicial Redress Act on February 12, 2016, and then-president Barack Obama signed it into law on February 24. The Judicial Redress Act, which amended the 1974 Privacy Act, allows the citizens of designated foreign countries or regional economic integration organizations to seek judicial redress before US courts in case the US authorities deny access or rectification or unlawfully disclose records transferred to the US (European Commission 2016g; Cîrlig 2016). It should be noted that this beyond-the-border extension of the scope of US judicial redress procedures is consistent with the EU's demand for the non-discriminatory treatment of EU citizens in terms of the availability of redress in the US.

A Global Approach to PNR Data Transfers

So far, the EU has signed bilateral PNR agreements with three countries: the US, Canada, and Australia. The EU–Canada PNR agreement was signed in 2006.[16] It allows the Canada Border Service Agency to obtain Advance Passenger Information (API) and PNR data from air carriers carrying passengers to Canada. The EU–Australia PNR agreements were signed in 2008[17] and 2012.[18] They provide for the transfer of EU-sourced PNR data by air carriers to the Australian Customs and Border Protection Service.

In addition, the EU has been negotiating with Mexico an agreement for the transfer of PNR data for the purposes of preventing terrorism and transnational organized crime since July 4, 2015[19] (European Commission 2015b). If concluded, the EU–Mexico PNR agreement would be the first of the "second-generation" PNR agreements that the EU makes with third countries, possibly followed by an agreement with Argentina.[20] A score of other third countries, including Russia, United Arab Emirates, South Korea, Brazil, Japan, and Saudi Arabia, have asked for the transfer of PNR data from the EU (Council of the EU 2015b).

Together with the "first-generation" agreements with the US, Canada, and Australia, future PNR accords may serve as a vehicle with which EU standards on the use of personal data for security purposes spread across the globe. Indeed, the EU seems to pursue global influence in this crucial area where counterterrorism and data protection policies intersect. In a communication of September 2010, the European Commission (2010) presented "the global approach to transfers of PNR data to third countries."[21] As a general consideration, the Commission states the following:

> Since the transmission, use and processing of PNR data affects the fundamental right of individuals to protection of their personal data, it is of central importance that the EU only cooperates with those third countries that can provide an adequate level of data protection for the EU originating PNR data (European Commission 2010, p. 7).

Such "an adequate level of data protection" would, in turn, be achieved by meeting the EU standards of data protection, which cover purpose limitation, sensitive data, data security, oversight and accountability, transparency and notice, access, rectification and deletion, redress, automated individual decisions, retention of data, restrictions on onward transfers to other government authorities, restrictions on onward transfers to third countries, and the method of transmission.[22]

Will the EU be the global standard-setter in the transfer and use of PNR data for law enforcement purposes? That remains to be seen. However, the chances are that the countries that request the transfer of PNR data from the EU—which are likely to increase in the future—would willingly or unwillingly take into account EU data protection principles and have them reflected in agreements with the EU.

Conclusion

The EU–US negotiations and the resulting agreements on PNR data transfer and use exhibit how the EU has dealt with the extraterritorial reach of US counterterrorism regulations. It may be argued that the EU adapted to US counterterrorism measures by agreeing to make EU-originating air passenger information available to US authorities. However, the EU did not simply subordinate itself to the security rules that the US unilaterally strengthened. Rather, the EU as a "receptive state" negotiated with the US and sought to establish a framework for "legal" transfer of EU-originating personal data that is consistent with European data protection principles.

Significantly, the EU–US PNR agreements set out rules and conditions that would in effect limit US authorities' use of PNR data originating in the EU. Furthermore, the EU sought to bring the crucial part of transfer operations within its jurisdiction and recently has had moderate success in this respect. Presumably, such conditions would prevent (or at least reduce) "disproportionate and excessive" use of EU-originating personal data by US authorities and mitigate the undermining effects of US extraterritorial regulations on the integrity of the European data protection regime.

A twist is that the EU's efforts to shelter its internal regime from external impact effectively resulted in the extraterritorial application of European privacy rules, particularly the EU Data Protection Directive. In essence, the EU through negotiations induced the US to make changes in its information practices that it would not have done otherwise. It may be, therefore, argued that the European data privacy regime became a source of EU influence over US security practices as the EU assumed both the receptive and assertive roles.

The EU is likely to continue to play an assertive role in the PNR matter, promoting the European standards on the transfer and use of PNR data for law enforcement purposes. Future PNR agreements between the EU and other jurisdictions will possibly be a means by which EU standards spread globally. The spread of EU standards, in turn, will have major implications for cross-border information exchange—a vital part of the war on transnational terrorism.

Notes

1 It should be stressed that the US requirement to submit PNR data caused controversy not because it was an attempt to promote information sharing but because it involved *personal* data. A comparison of the PNR dispute with the low-profile case of the Container Security Initiative (CSI) may illustrate this point (Suda 2013). Announced in January 2002, the CSI is intended to address the threat posed by potential terrorist use of a maritime cargo container by identifying high-risk containers before they are shipped to the US (US Customs and Border Protection 2008). In connection with the CSI, the US government proposed that carriers electronically provide its customs with cargo manifest information 24 hours before the related cargo is loaded on board a ship destined for the US. Despite the intrusive character of the CSI, the EU in April 2004 made an agreement with the US that provided for the exchange of relevant information with the US as well as accommodating the US in deploying its customs officials at European ports. Unlike the PNR agreements, the EU–US CSI agreement has not caused major controversy until today, because information sharing under the CSI does not involve *personal* data, and, therefore, it is not a part of the grand debate about an appropriate balance between civil liberty and national security.

2 The European Commission took the view that PNR data should be used if they were shown to make a difference (interview with a European Commission official, June 3, 2010).

3 The Council of the EU is the institution representing the member states' governments. Also known informally as the EU Council, it is where national ministers from each EU country meet to adopt laws and coordinate policies. The website of the Council of the EU, www.consilium.europa.eu/en/council-eu/, accessed April 14, 2017.

4 Under the Maastricht Treaty (Treaty on European Union), which entered into force on November 1, 1993, the EU as an institution was based on three groups

of powers that were commonly referred to as "pillars." The "first pillar" consisted of the European Communities, providing a framework within which the single market functioned. The "second pillar" was the Common Foreign and Security Policy (CFSP). The "third pillar" was cooperation in the fields of justice and home affairs (JHA). See European Parliament (2016).

5 In the Declaration on Combating Terrorism, adopted in March 2004 shortly after the terrorist bombings in Madrid, the European Council called for legal measures to use air passenger data as a part of efforts to strengthen border controls and document security.

6 Among the information contained in PNR, choice of meals falls into the category of sensitive data as it might indicate religious affiliation of a passenger.

7 Under the 2007 agreement, however, sensitive data may be used in an exceptional case where the life of a data subject or of others could be imperiled or seriously impaired. This may be seen as a setback (Newman 2011).

8 The 2004 agreement included the application of the US Freedom of Information Act (FOIA) to non-US citizens, and the 2007 agreement provided for the extension of protection under the US Privacy Act of 1974 to PNR data stored in the database of US authorities regardless of the nationality or country of residence of the data subject. This was a major improvement from the initial condition, in which individuals had no right to review or correct the stored data.

9 It should be noted that the European data protection regulators did not resist the transfer of PNR data *per se* but were skeptical of what they saw as an extensive use of PNR in the US (Newman 2011).

10 Similarly to the 2007 agreement, however, access to, as well as processing and use of, sensitive data would be permitted in exceptional circumstances where the life of an individual could be imperiled or seriously impaired.

11 The 2012 PNR agreement reads, "For the purposes of this Agreement, carriers shall be required to transfer PNR to DHS using the 'push' method, in furtherance of the need for accuracy, timeliness and completeness of PNR."

12 The Department of Homeland Security contributed to the prolonged operation of the "pull" system by claiming to receive updated PNR data as necessary to ensure data accuracy. Since airlines wished to avoid the burden of having to "push" data whenever requested by the CBP, shift to a "push" system was slow.

13 Compared to a "pull" system, a "push" system causes more expense to airlines, which bear the costs to "push" data whenever the CBP requests. This suggests that request for a "push" system was made on normative rather than economic grounds.

14 In a resolution of March 26, 2009, the European Parliament stressed that the sharing of data and information with the US "must take place within a proper legal framework, ensuring adequate protection of civil liberties, including the right to privacy" and "should be based on a binding international agreement" (European Parliament 2009a, point 43). Subsequently, in December 2009, the European Council invited the European Commission to propose a recommendation "for the negotiation of a data protection and, where necessary, data sharing agreements for law enforcement purposes with the US" (European Commission 2016g).

15 In a communication titled "Rebuilding Trust in EU–US Data Flows," the European Commission argued that "the conclusion of such an [Umbrella] agreement providing for a high level of protection of personal data would represent a major contribution to strengthening trust across the Atlantic" (European Commission 2013b, point 3.3).

16 Agreement between the European Community and the Government of Canada on the processing of Advance Passenger Information and Passenger Name Record data.

17 Agreement between the European Union and Australia on the processing and transfer of European Union-sourced passenger name record (PNR) data by air carriers to the Australian customs service.
18 Agreement between the European Union and Australia on the processing and transfer of Passenger Name Record (PNR) data by air carriers to the Australian Customs and Border Protection Service.
19 Mexico adopted PNR legislation in 2012 requesting the transfer of passenger data from the air carriers that operate in the country (Council of the EU 2015b).
20 Argentina adopted PNR legislation on September 24, 2014 (Council of the EU 2015b).
21 This strategy was formulated upon the request of the European Parliament, which welcomed the document and then approved the launch of renegotiation of the PNR agreement.
22 As to the method of transmission, the Communication says, "To safeguard the data that is contained in the carriers' databases and to maintain their control thereof, data should be transmitted using exclusively the 'push' system."

6 The EU PNR Directive

While negotiating with the United States (US), the European Union (EU) has developed its own policy on the use of passenger name records (PNRs) for law enforcement purposes. The development of the EU's PNR policy was driven by terrorist attacks in the EU, but it also has been influenced by the EU–US talks and the resulting agreements over the transfer of PNR data. The policy process regarding an EU PNR system started in the mid-2000s and, after a long debate, culminated in the adoption of the EU PNR Directive in April 2016.

Initiative by the Council

Like the US, the EU's policy to use PNR data for law enforcement purposes has evolved in the context of preventing and combating terrorism. Early calls for an EU-wide policy to use PNR data were found in counterterrorism initiatives by the Council.

On March 25, 2004, the European Council[1] adopted the Declaration on Combating Terrorism in the wake of the Madrid Bombings of March 11. In the declaration, the Council called for, among other things, strengthened border controls. As a part of this effort, it invited the European Commission to "bring forward a proposal no later than June 2004 for a common EU approach to the use of passengers [*sic*] data for border and aviation security and other law enforcement purposes" (European Council 2004, point 6).

The Council reiterated its invitation to the Commission to bring forward a proposal for a common EU approach to the use of air passenger data for law enforcement purposes in the Hague Programme, which was adopted at the European Council of November 4 and 5, 2004, with a view to strengthening freedom, security, and justice in the EU (European Council 2005, point 2.2). Furthermore, on July 13, 2005, the Council for the second time reiterated the request for a PNR proposal in the Declaration on the EU Response to the London Bombings of July 7, 2005. Stressing "the need to reduce vulnerability to attack by protecting citizens and infrastructure," the Council called on the European Commission to "bring forward the proposal on air line [*sic*] passenger name records by October 2005" (Council of the European Union 2005, point 6).[2]

European Commission's "Global EU Approach"

For its part, the European Commission had announced a European policy in the area of air passenger information *before* the European Council adopted the Declaration on Combating Terrorism. On December 16, 2003, the European Commission brought out a communication titled "Transfer of Air Passenger Name Record (PNR) Data: A global EU approach" against the background of the EU–US talks on PNR data transfer (European Commission 2003d). In the communication, the Commission argued that one of the main components of the "global EU approach" was the "development of an EU position on the use of travellers' data, including PNR, for aviation and border security." The Commission stated as follows:

> The talks with third countries on the transfer of PNR data should be complemented and to the extent possible preceded by the development of an EU policy on the use of PNR and/or travellers' data more generally within the Union. Such a policy will have to strike a balance between the different interests involved, in particular between legitimate security concerns and the protection of fundamental rights, including privacy.
>
> (European Commission 2003d, point 3.4)

Proposal for a Council Framework Decision

On November 6, 2007, the European Commission adopted a proposal for a Council Framework Decision on the use of PNR data for law enforcement purposes (European Commission 2007c). In essence, the proposed Framework Decision provides for the "making available by air carriers of PNR data of passengers of international flights to the competent authorities of the Member State, for the purpose of preventing and combating terrorist offences and organised crime" (Article 1).

More specifically, the proposed Framework Decision provided that air carriers should make 19 PNR data elements available to what are called "Passenger Information Units" (PIUs) of the member states through the "push" method. No "special categories of personal data" (i.e. sensitive data) would be used. PIUs would retain data for a period of five years in an active database and then for a further period of eight years in a dormant database (European Commission 2007c).

European data protection authorities examined the proposal with substantial caution as the proposed Framework Decision would have a major impact on privacy. Article 29 Data Protection Working Party and Working Party on Police and Justice (2007) jointly released an opinion on the proposal, arguing that the necessity and proportionality of the proposal were problematic. "If the current version of the draft Framework Decision is implemented," claimed the Working Parties, "Europe would take a great leap forwards towards a complete surveillance society making all travellers suspects" (p. 13). The European Data Protection Supervisor (EDPS) (2007b) also expressed serious concerns about the necessity and proportionality of the proposal, which in his view were not sufficiently established.[3]

Such a cautious view was shared with the European Parliament. In a resolution of November 2008, the Parliament made strong reservations as to the necessity of the proposal as well as the proportionality of the measures (European Parliament 2008).

The debate over the proposal for a Framework Decision on the use of PNR data was truncated with the entry into force of the Treaty of Lisbon on December 1, 2009. As the Council did not adopt the proposed Framework Decision by that time, the proposal became obsolete.

Under the post-Lisbon institutional arrangement, an EU PNR scheme was to be established through a co-decision procedure, whereby the Council of the EU and the European Parliament would legislate together. This means that the European Parliament became able to play a larger role in the development of the EU's PNR policy.

Proposal for an EU PNR Scheme

Discussions on a possible PNR scheme within the EU continued despite the abandonment of the proposal for a Council Framework Decision. The Stockholm Programme, adopted by the European Council in December 2009, called on the European Commission to present a proposal for the use of PNR data for the purpose of preventing, detecting, investigating, and prosecuting terrorist offences and serious crime, with a view to setting up an EU PNR system (European Council 2010). Meanwhile, the European Commission expressed its intention to replace the obsolete proposal for a Framework Decision with a new proposal for a directive for the use of PNR data for law enforcement purposes in its communication of September 21, 2010, titled "On the global approach to transfers of passenger name record (PNR) data to third countries" (European Commission 2010).

On February 2, 2011, the Commission adopted a proposal for a directive on the use of PNR data for the prevention, detection, investigation, and prosecution of terrorist offences and serious crime. The proposed directive provided for the transfer by air carriers of PNR data of international air passengers to and from the member states (i.e. extra-EU flights), as well as the processing of PNR data. Similar to the proposed Framework Decision, the proposed directive would require the member states to set up a PIU and adopt measures to ensure that air carriers would transfer (i.e. "push") PNR data to PIUs. Also similar to the Framework Decision proposal, the proposed directive provided that 19 elements of PNR data would be collected, with the processing of sensitive data prohibited. However, the period of data retention was shorter in the proposed directive than in the proposed Framework Decision; it provided that the PNR data transferred would be retained in a PIU database for 30 days, and, after that, the data would be "masked out" (i.e. stripped of all data elements that could serve to identify the passenger) and retained at PIUs for a further period of five years (European Commission 2011d).

The Council of the EU, in its meeting in April 2012, agreed to a general approach on the draft directive, allowing for the beginning of negotiations with the European Parliament under the co-decision procedure (Council of the EU 2012). In agreeing on a general approach, the Council proposed two changes in the draft. First, while the Commission's proposal was limited to the collection of PNR data for extra-EU flights, the Council proposed that the new rules would allow, but not oblige, member states to also collect PNR data concerning selected intra-EU fights (i.e. flights from an EU member state to another EU member state). Second, the Council proposed that the collected PNR data would be masked out after two years, instead of 30 days as provided in the Commission's proposal.

The European Parliament, however, remained cautious about the establishment of an EU PNR system. In April 2013, the Parliament's Civil Liberties (LIBE) Committee rejected the draft directive by a narrow majority. The major points debated at the time included, *inter alia*, the necessity and proportionality of the directive, its scope, and the length of the data retention period. Subsequently, in June 2013, the Parliament decided in plenary session to refer the matter back to the LIBE Committee. It should be noted that, by doing so, the Parliament did not scrap the proposal for an EU PNR directive, but chose to continue the work in search of an agreement (European Parliament 2016d; and Voronova 2015).

Necessity and Proportionality

As was the case with the EU–US PNR agreements, the debate over the EU PNR scheme centered on the questions of the necessity and proportionality of the proposal and its compliance with fundamental rights. It should be recalled that Article 8 of the European Convention on Human Rights provides that limitation of rights to privacy is allowed only when the measures are necessary and proportionate. Thus, EDPS has argued as follows:

> the demonstration of the necessity and the proportionality of the data processing is an absolute prerequisite for the development of the PNR scheme. The EU needs to justify on a basis of available evidence why a massive, non-targeted and indiscriminate collection of data of individuals is necessary and why that measure is urgently needed.
>
> (EDPS 2015, point 10)

In the opinion of EDPS, there was a lack of information to justify why and how the establishment of an EU PNR scheme was necessary to achieve the purposes of preventing, detecting, investigating, and prosecuting terrorist offences and serious crime. Furthermore, in the view of EDPS, the measures proposed did not appear as proportionate to the objective of the EU PNR scheme. In particular, the bulk and indiscriminate collection of data, lengthy data retention period,[4] and lack of objective criteria to determine the limits of the competent authorities' access to data seemed to be inconsistent with the principle of proportionality (EDPS 2015).

Revival of the EU PNR Proposal

While the procedure to legislate an EU PNR directive had been blocked, the proposal on the use of PNR data came back under the spotlight after the terrorist attack in Paris on January 7, 2015. Since the Paris attack, the fight against terrorism and the phenomenon of "foreign fighters" (Europeans returning home after fighting abroad for terrorist groups) have reached the top of the EU agenda, leading to renewed discussions of measures to counter the perceived terrorist threat. It was in this new security context that the EU PNR proposal was refocused and revived (Bąkowski and Voronova 2015; European Parliament 2016d).

Along with the concerned member states, the Council renewed its call for an EU-wide system to use PNR data for law enforcement purposes (Bąkowski and Voronova 2015). In a statement on February 12, 2015, the European Council asked that EU legislators urgently adopt a strong and effective EU PNR directive with solid data protection safeguards (European Council 2015).

The European Parliament followed the calls. In a resolution of February 11, 2015, on anti-terrorism measures, the Parliament committed itself "to work towards the finalization of an EU PNR Directive by the end of the year" (European Parliament 2015b, point 13).[5] The Parliament reiterated its commitment in its resolution on the European Agenda on Security, which was passed on July 9, 2015, as well as its resolution on the prevention of radicalization and recruitment of European citizens by terrorist organizations, which was adopted on November 25, 2015, in the wake of the November 13 Paris terrorist attacks.

In finalizing the directive, the Parliament—to be precise, the LIBE Committee— proposed a number of amendments in the draft text. The revised text was approved by the committee on July 15, 2015. According to the text, the amended PNR rules would apply to air carriers operating "international flights" (i.e. extra-EU flights) and would not apply to "intra-EU flights." Under the amended rules, PNR data could be processed only for the purposes of prevention, detection, investigation, and prosecution of terrorist offences and certain types of "serious *transnational* crime" (rather than "serious crime"). PNR data transferred to a PIU would be retained for an initial period of 30 days and then "masked out" and retained for up to four years in serious transnational crime cases and five years for terrorism; after the five years, PNR data would have to be permanently deleted. Furthermore, the amended rules contained data protection safeguards, including limitation of the purposes for which PNR data could be processed at PIUs, appointment of a data protection officer in PIUs, logging or documenting of all processing of PNR data, and stricter conditions on the transfer of data to third countries (European Parliament 2016d).

Having revised the draft directive, the Parliament entered into the three-way negotiations ("trilogues") with the Council and the Commission on September 24, 2015 (European Parliament 2016d). The November 2015 Paris terrorist attacks gave added impetus to a compromise (Monteleone 2016).

On December 2, 2015, the Parliament and the Council reached a provisional agreement on an EU PNR Directive. The agreed text of the directive was approved by the Parliament during a plenary session on April 14, 2016.[6] It was then approved by the Council of the EU on April 21, 2016. Member states will have two years to transpose the directive into their national laws[7] (European Parliament 2016d).

The EU PNR Directive

The adopted EU PNR Directive is not radically different from the original proposal. Similar to the Commission's proposal, the directive provides for the collection of 19 elements of PNR data (Annex I), and explicitly prohibits the processing of sensitive data (Article 13). PNR data collected in accordance with the directive may be processed only for the purposes of preventing, investigating, and prosecuting terrorist offences and serious crime[8] (Article 1). The members states are responsible for establishing a PIU, which in turn is responsible for collecting, storing, and processing PNR data; for transferring data to the competent authorities; and for exchanging data with the PIUs of other member states and with Europol (Article 4). Air carriers are obliged to transfer, by the "push method," PNR data to PIU databases of the member states (Article 8). Sharing of PNR data between PIUs and with Europol may take place if the transfer is "necessary for a specific case of prevention, detection, investigation or prosecution of terrorist offences or serious crime" (articles 9 and 10). Transfer of PNR data to third countries may be made "only on a case-by-case basis" and if the transfer is "necessary" for the purposes of preventing, detecting, investigating, and prosecuting terrorist offences and serious crime (Article 11).[9] With regard to the protection of personal data, the directive grants passengers rights to protection of their personal data, rights of access, rectification, erasure, and restriction, and rights to compensation and judicial redress (Article 13).

The EU PNR Directive, nonetheless, is different from the proposal in the scope of application. While providing for the transfer by air carriers of

PNR data of passengers of extra-EU flights (Article 1), the directive may also be applied to selected intra-EU flights upon notification to the Commission (Article 2). As noted, the inclusion of intra-EU flights was proposed by the Council, but was not supported by the Parliament.

Another difference was the period of data retention and depersonalization. Under the PNR Directive, PNR data transferred to PIUs will be retained in their databases for a period of five years.[10] However, after six months of storage, the data will be depersonalized through masking out elements such as names, addresses, and contact information that may lead to the identification of the passenger to whom the PNR data relate.[11] In other words, the retention period of full PNR data has been prolonged from the original proposal's 30 days to six months (although it is still shorter than the period the Council proposed, i.e. two years).

On the other hand, the PNR Directive has additional data protection safeguards in line with the amendments the Parliament proposed. They include the appointment of a data protection officer in the PIU (Article 5) and documentation of PIUs' data-processing operations (Article 13).

Influence of the EU–US PNR Negotiations and Agreements

The EU's PNR policy was developed in parallel with the EU–US negotiations over the transfer of PNR data from the EU to the US. The influence of the negotiations can be seen in the proposal for a Council Framework Decision on the use of PNR data, which was "closely modelled on the 2007 EU–US PNR agreement" (Article 29 Data Protection Working Party and Working Party on Police and Justice 2007, p. 2). The proposal, indeed, was "in a number of areas almost the exact mirror of the transatlantic PNR system" (Argomaniz 2009, p. 130). Both schemes would collect 19 very similar elements of PNR data for the purposes of combating terrorist offences and serious (transnational) crimes. In both schemes, the collected data would be retained for an initial period of five years in an "active" database (however, while the 2007 agreement provides for the further retention of data in a "dormant" database for the period of ten years, the proposed Framework Decision provides for the further retention period of eight years). Both schemes would prohibit the use of sensitive data. Finally, while the proposed Framework Decision provides that PNRs would be transferred to PIUs by the "push" method, the 2007 agreement provides that PNR data will be *eventually* sent ("pushed") by airlines (see Pawlak 2009b).

Such similarities are hardly surprising, because—as discussed in the previous chapter—the EU–US PNR agreements at least partially reflect the preferences of the EU. It should be recalled that, under the 2007 agreement, fewer elements of PNR data would be collected than the US had initially proposed, for the purposes of dealing with a narrower range of criminal offences than the US had originally requested, and these would be retained for a shorter period of time than the US had sought. It should also be recalled that the definition of sensitive data was derived directly from the EU Data Protection Directive, and that the "push" method was the choice of the EU, rather than the US.

It may be argued, nevertheless, that the 2016 EU PNR Directive has been influenced by the negotiations with the US to the extent that there are similarities between the directive and the 2012 EU–US PNR agreement. In fact, the directive and the agreement are very similar in the types of data collected and the purposes for which those data are used. However, the retention period provided by the 2016 Directive—one of its key features—is different from the EU–US agreement. While the 2012 EU–US PNR agreement provides that data are retained in an "active" database for up to five years, and then transferred to a "dormant" database for a period of up to ten years, the 2016 EU PNR Directive provides that data are retained for five years, with full data only preserved during the first 60 days.

Arguably, the most important influence from the US is the demonstration effect of the US PNR policy and practices. It should be stressed that the European Commission's evaluation of the necessity of an EU PNR scheme was based on the US PNR framework. The explanatory memorandum of the proposal for the Council Framework Decision states as follows:

> Currently, arrangements for the transmission of PNR data in the context of the fight against terrorism and transnational organised crime have been concluded between the EU and the United States and Canada and are limited to travel by air. These require that air carriers, which were already capturing the PNR data of passengers for their own commercial purposes, are obliged to transmit these data to the competent authorities of the USA and Canada. *On the basis of an exchange of information with* these third countries, the EU has been able to assess the value of PNR data and to *realise its potential for law enforcement purposes*.
>
> (European Commission 2007c, p. 2, italics added)

At the same time, the memorandum states as follows:

> The EU has further been able to learn from the experiences of such third countries in the use of PNR data, as well as from the experience of the UK from its pilot project. More specifically, the UK was able to report numerous arrests, identification of human trafficking networks and gaining of valuable intelligence in relation to terrorism in the two years of the operation of its pilot project.
>
> (European Commission 2007c, p. 2)

In other words, the European Commission "learned" not only from the experiences of third countries, namely the US and Canada, but also from member states of the EU, namely the United Kingdom (UK).

National PNR Systems in EU Member States

It is important to note that the EU PNR Directive addresses the problem of harmonization among EU member states' PNR policies by establishing EU-wide common rules. Such harmonization has been called for because some member states have set up their own PNR systems, while others have enacted legislation to use PNR data for law enforcement purposes.

In 2011, at the time the EU PNR Directive was proposed, only the UK had a full-fledged PNR system. Since 2004, under the Semaphore project, PNR data had already been collected and used by UK law enforcement authorities to combat crime and terrorism as well as for immigration control. However, the UK is not alone in the collection and use of PNR data. Denmark has legislation to access PNR data for external border control and antiterrorism investigations. Belgium has been using PNR data for many years, but only on a case-by-case basis in the context of criminal investigations (Bąkowski and Voronova 2015).[12]

Such piecemeal development of national PNR systems raises concern at EU level because it would result in divergent standards on the collection and processing of PNR data across the EU. Thus, an EU-wide regulation that establishes common standards is called for; by following the common standards, member states will harmonize their PNR policies, filling potential gaps in security and data protection practices. In this sense, the EU PNR Directive is an EU response to the patchy development of national PNR systems in European countries.

Conclusion

The EU PNR Directive would require more systematic collection, use, and retention of air passengers' personal data and thus have an impact on the rights to privacy and data protection (European Parliament 2016d). The controversial EU PNR scheme emerged and gained momentum after major terrorist incidents in Europe, namely the 2004 Madrid bombings, 2005 London bombings, and 2015 Paris terrorist attacks. It may be, therefore, argued that the EU PNR system was developed to mitigate the threat of terrorism, particularly acts of terror by "foreign fighters."

However, terrorist incidents themselves do not justify the collection and use of air passengers' personal data for law enforcement purposes. Importantly, the argument for the necessity of an EU PNR scheme—made by the European Commission—was based on the experiences of the US PNR framework *and* the UK PNR program.

The details of the EU PNR system were discussed in light of the proportionality principle. In other words, various elements of the system were debated—most notably in the European Parliament—to make the use of PNR data proportionate to the purpose (i.e. counterterrorism and law enforcement). This resulted in the EU standards for the collection, use, and processing of PNR data, which might serve as a baseline for future PNR agreements the EU makes with third countries.

The EU PNR system is scheduled to come into operation in 2018. Meanwhile the debate over the system, particularly regarding its necessity and proportionality, is likely to continue in Europe.

Notes

1 The European Council is the EU institution that defines the general political direction and priorities of the European Union. It consists of the heads of state or government of the member states, together with its president and the president of the European Commission. The website of the European Council, www.consilium.europa.eu/en/european-council/president/, accessed April 14, 2017.

2 It should be noted that the idea of using air passenger information for law enforcement purposes was not new. In accordance with Directive 2004/82/EC of April 29, 2004, air carriers transporting passengers into the territory of EU member states were obliged to transfer advance passenger information (API), such as the number and type of travel document used, nationality, full names, and the date of birth, to competent national authorities in order to improve border control and combat illegal immigration.

3 In raising the question of necessity, both the working parties and EDPS referred to the existence of the EU API system.

4 With regard to data retention period, EDPS referred to the European Court of Justice's judgment of April 8, 2014, which had declared that the Data Retention Directive was invalid. In this judgment, the Court held that "the determination of the period of retention must be based on objective criteria in order to ensure that it is limited to what is necessary" (EDPS 2015).

5 In the resolution, the Parliament urged the Commission to set out the possible impact of the EU's Court of Justice Data Retention judgment on the PNR proposal. Furthermore, it encouraged the Council to make progress on the Data Protection Package, so that trilogues on both the EU PNR Directive and the Data Protection Package could take place in parallel.

6 The text of the directive was approved by 461 votes to 179, with nine abstentions (European Parliament 2016d).

7 The United Kingdom and Ireland have opted in to the EU PNR Directive, while Denmark is not participating (European Parliament 2016d).

8 This means that, despite the Parliament's proposal, the scope was not narrowed to cover terrorism and serious "transnational" crime.

9 Transfer of PNR data to third countries is also subject to the conditions laid down in Article 13 of the Council Framework Decision 2008/977/JHA of 27 November 2008 on the protection of personal data processed in the framework of police and judicial cooperation in criminal matters.

10 This means that the total retention period under the directive is 30 days shorter than the Commission's proposal (i.e. five years and 30 days).

11 After the initial period of six months, disclosure of the full PNR data will be permitted only where it is "reasonably believed" that it is necessary for the purposes of carrying out an assessment of passengers prior to their arrival (Article 12).

12 It is noteworthy that the European Commission has actively promoted the development of national PNR systems in member states. In 2013, 50 million euro, made available by the Commission under its "Prevention of and Fight against Crime" program, was distributed between 14 member states, which proposed developing national PNR systems (Bąkowski and Voronova 2015).

7 The SWIFT Affair

Like the disputes over passenger name records (PNRs), the transatlantic row over financial transactions records held by the Society for Worldwide Interbank Financial Transactions (SWIFT) stemmed from the United States (US) government's response to the events of September 11, 2001. Indeed, the SWIFT affair is yet "another instance of the extraterritorial reach of American anti-terrorist policies" (Kahler and Lake 2009, p. 266).

It may be argued that, to some extent, combating terrorist financing must be international in scope as terrorists take advantage of money flows across borders to support their operations (e.g. to acquire weapons, recruit new members, arrange travels, and stage attacks). However, extensive surveillance of international money flows by US authorities—which were involved in gathering information on financial transactions conducted *outside* as well as within the US—concerned the privacy of, among others, hundreds of thousands of European citizens and thus created tensions with the European Union (EU).

US TFTP

Shortly after the terrorist attacks of September 11, the US Department of the Treasury initiated the Terrorist Finance Tracking Program (TFTP) to identify, track, and pursue terrorists and their networks (US Department of the Treasury n.d.). As part of this mission, the Treasury Department's Office of Foreign Assets Control (OFAC) began to issue administrative subpoenas on SWIFT to obtain financial transaction information on individuals and/or entities suspected to be related to terrorist activities. If SWIFT declined, it would run the risk of incurring sanctions under US law.

SWIFT thus complied with the Treasury Department's subpoenas early on, allowing US authorities access to its data through a "black box" arrangement. This means that data were not extracted or searched by SWIFT but transferred in "bulk." As a matter of procedures, the Treasury instructed SWIFT to provide broadly defined categories of information on financial transactions relating to "*x* number of countries and jurisdictions" on "*y* date" or "*from* … *to* …" (dates ranging from one to several weeks). Once transferred, data were analyzed with the help of automated software to find links between terrorists and their supporters (Article 29 Working Party 2006; de Goede 2012a).

SWIFT is an industry-owned co-operative that provides an international messaging service between financial institutions (mainly but not limited to banks). Headquartered in La Hulpe, Belgium, SWIFT processes approximately 80 percent of financial transactions of the world through its global network[1]. For reasons of data security, SWIFT used to store and process all financial messages (i.e. electronic payment instructions) at two operating centers, one in Europe and the other in the US. On these sites SWIFT operated two identical "mirror" servers, which functioned as each other's "back-up." Financial transaction data were stored in each server for 124 days and then erased (Article 29 Working Party 2006; European Commission 2007b).

Legally speaking, the TFTP is based on US Presidential Executive Order 13224 of September 23, 2001, which purports to disrupt the financial support network for terrorists and terrorist organizations and authorizes notably the Treasury Department to employ all powers granted to the president by the International Emergency Economic Powers Act of 1977 (IEEPA)[2] and the United Nations Participation Act of 1945 (UNPA)[3] as may be necessary to carry out the purposes of the order. If a financial institution fails to produce the information requested by a subpoena, it faces possible criminal and civil penalties, including seizure of assets (Santolli 2008). Notwithstanding their legal basis, however, TFTP operations were conducted in great secrecy and did not come to public light until June 2006, when the *New York Times* revealed the existence of the program (Lichtblau and Risen 2006).

To be precise, the Treasury Department's subpoenas asked SWIFT's American operating center to turn over data held on the "mirror" server *in the US*. The subpoenaed information, however, might include data that had originated in the SWIFT server *in Europe* and related to financial transactions *outside* the US, including transactions that took place entirely within Europe.

It should be noted that the Treasury Department could exert regulatory authority over SWIFT through subpoenas precisely because SWIFT had an office within the jurisdiction of the US. In other words, the very existence of a branch office in US territory made SWIFT vulnerable to sanctions that could be imposed by the Treasury for noncompliance. SWIFT in turn has located one of its operation centers in the US presumably to take advantage of the huge US financial market. It may be argued, therefore, that the US regulatory authorities indirectly benefited from the tremendous size and importance of the US capital market (see Kahler and Lake 2009).

Outcry in the EU

The disclosure of the TFTP sparked substantial controversy on both sides of the Atlantic (de Goede 2012a).

In the EU, controversy focused on privacy issues, because the transferred data might contain personally identifiable information, such as names, bank account numbers, addresses, and national identification numbers of payers and recipients. A barrage of criticism was set off, questioning the legitimacy of US officials' access to private financial data of European citizens (de Goede 2012a).

Data protection authorities spearheaded the criticism against the TFTP. The Privacy Commission of Belgium, where SWIFT has its headquarters, decided in September 2006 that the transfer by SWIFT of personal data to SWIFT's US branch breached the Belgian data protection law and accused SWIFT of a "hidden systematic, massive and long-term violation of the fundamental European principles as regards data protection" (Article 29 Working Party 2006, p. 7).[4]

At the EU level, the Article 29 Working Party in November 2006 issued an opinion which found that "the hidden, systematic, massive and long-term transfer of personal data by SWIFT to the UST [US Treasury] … constitutes a violation of fundamental European principles as regards data protection and is not in accordance with Belgian and European law" (Article 29 Working Party 2006, p. 26). The Working Party pointed out that:

- while originally collected for a commercial purpose (i.e. transactions between financial institutions), the subpoenaed data were processed for a further, incompatible purpose (i.e. tracking terrorist financing) in violation of the data quality principle stipulated in Article 6 of the EU Data Protection Directive;
- SWIFT (and the financial institutions in the EU) failed to inform data subjects about the further processing of their personal data and thus to comply with the notification requirements provided in Articles 18 to 20 of the Directive; and
- SWIFT failed to provide an appropriate level of protection in order to meet the requirements for international transfers of personal data set forth in Article 25 of the Directive.(Article 29 Working Party 2006)

The European Data Protection Supervisor (EDPS) also expressed his disapproval of the data transfer, saying that "[s]ecret, routine and massive access of third country authorities to banking data is unacceptable" (EDPS 2007b, paragraph 2). The EDPS called on the European Central Bank (ECB) to take measures as SWIFT is subject to cooperative oversight by the central banks of Group of Ten countries, including the ECB. However, the ECB refused to get involved in the matter, claiming that SWIFT's compliance with the Treasury's subpoenas was outside its competence (Article 29 Working Party 2006; EDPS 2007a).

The European Parliament proved the ally of data protection authorities. In July 2006, the Parliament adopted a resolution on the interception of bank transfer data from the SWIFT system to the US secret services.

Stressing that "all transfers of personal data to third countries are subject to data protection legislation at national and European level," the resolution demanded that "the Member States check whether and ensure that there is no legal lacuna at national level" (European Parliament 2006, 2 and 8). In addition, the resolution raised questions over the purpose of the use of the transferred data. As SWIFT data contained information on the economic activities of individuals and countries, it was suspected that the data transfer operations would possibly give rise to "large-scale forms of economic and industrial espionage" (European Parliament 2006, D).

The US Representations

With these strong rebukes, it was not a viable option for the European Council or the European Commission to acquiesce to the "illegal state of affairs" (Article 29 Working Party 2006, p. 2). However, neither was it practical for them to block transfer of SWIFT data for the purpose of the TFTP as the EU was committed to the fight against terrorist financing. Indeed, in its Declaration on Combating Terrorism of March 2004, the European Council stated that it believed that "strong preventive action must continue to be taken on the sources of financing of terrorist organisations and to swiftly disrupt the flow of financial resources to terrorist groups and related entities and individuals, while respecting the rule of law" (Council of the European Union 2004, point 10). The EU-US Declaration on Combating Terrorism of June 2004 reaffirmed this commitment "to prevent access by terrorists to financial and other economic resources" (Council of the European Union 2004b, point 2).

Accordingly, the Council Presidency, supported by the European Commission, sought a legally acceptable solution in the "letter exchange" format that had been devised in the PNR talks (De Hert and Bellanova 2008). In January 2007, the European Commission announced that it had begun informal talks with the US government (Fuster et al. 2008).

With European prompting, the Treasury Department in June 2007 gave a set of unilateral commitments called "representations"—a functional equivalent of US "undertakings" of the PNR package—in a letter to the EU Council Presidency and the European Commission. The US representations, in essence, described the controls and safeguards governing the handling, use and dissemination of data received from SWIFT under the TFTP[5]. Specifically, the US gave assurances that:

- the transferred data were used exclusively for counterterrorism purposes (i.e. not for other purposes, such as investigation of tax evasion);
- the TFTP did not involve data mining or other type of algorithmic or automated profiling or computer-filtering;
- non-extracted (non-used) data would be deleted not later than five years after receipt;

- data were maintained in a secure environment;
- the subpoenas served upon SWIFT were carefully and narrowly tailored to limit the amount of data transferred to the Treasury Department;
- appropriate redress for possible misuse by US government authorities would be available under US law; and
- "[a]s a sign of our commitment and partnership in combating global terrorism," an "eminent European person" would be appointed to confirm that the TFTP was implemented consistent with the representations.[6]

In a reply letter, the EU Council Presidency and the European Commission expressed their appreciation for the opportunity the Treasury Department had given the EU "to have its views and concerns duly reflected in the representations" and affirmed that "once SWIFT and the financial institutions making use of its services have completed the necessary arrangements" they "will be in compliance with their respective legal responsibilities under European data protection law." In the words of Franco Frattini, vice-president of the Commission, the European Commission considered the "representations" to provide "the necessary guarantees that U.S. Treasury processes data it receives from Swift's [*sic*] mirror server in USA in a way which takes account of EU data protection principles" (European Commission 2007a).

Meanwhile SWIFT decided to sign up for the Safe Harbor privacy program of the US Department of Commerce in a bid to assure that data located in the US operating center would be protected under similar data protection principles as in Europe (SWIFT 2007b). While not specifically designed to cover financial institutions, Safe Harbor nonetheless was considered the "only" scheme that provided for an adequate level of protection for data transfers from the EU to US organizations (Article 29 Working Party 2006).

Re-architecture of the SWIFT Network

The case was not settled, however. In June 2007, SWIFT announced, presumably under pressure from the Belgian data protection authority, a plan to redesign the architecture of its messaging network and build a new operating center in Switzerland. The stated aims of the re-architecture were to expand messaging capacity, reinforce network resilience, and "allay data privacy concerns raised in the context of SWIFT's required compliance with US subpoenas for subsets of SWIFT messages" (SWIFT 2007a). Under the plan, SWIFT would create two message-processing zones: European and Transatlantic. In this multi-zonal architecture, messages in the European processing zones, including messages internal to the European Economic Area (EEA) and Switzerland, would be processed and stored in both the existing European operation center and the new Swiss operation center. Intra-European messages then would remain in Europe, "thereby overcoming data protection concerns" (SWIFT 2007c). The new messaging structure was to be operational by the end of 2009.

The plan for a system re-architecture, however, raised concerns in the US as it meant that intra-European financial transaction data would no longer be "mirrored" in the US operating center. This would be a major blow to the TFTP. If data originating from Europe were not transferred to the US server, a substantial part of SWIFT data would stay outside the scope of the Treasury Department's subpoenas.

To maintain the TFTP's access to financial records of *all* regions of the world, the US government sought an arrangement with the EU on the transfer of SWIFT data from Europe. The EU Council and the European Commission concurred in the belief that the TFTP generated valuable information for the fight against terror and that the TFTP was important for European security. According to the Council, by 2009, the TFTP passed more than 1450 leads to European governments, which were used in the investigation of many terrorist attacks and attempted attacks, including the Al-Qa'ida-directed liquid bomb plot against transatlantic aircraft in 2006 (General Secretariat of the Council of the EU 2009).

The European Parliament, for its part, adopted a resolution in September 2009 that demanded that the envisaged agreement with the US must, at a minimum, ensure that:

> a data are transferred and processed only for the purposes of fighting terrorism, and that they relate to individuals or terrorist organisations recognised as such also by the EU;
>
> b the processing of such data as regards their transfer (only by means of a 'push' system), storage and use is not disproportionate to the objective for which those data have been transferred and are subsequently processed;
>
> c the transfer requests are based on specific, targeted cases, limited in time and subject to judicial authorisation, and that any subsequent processing is limited to data which disclose a link with persons or organisations under examination in the US; that data which do not disclose such links are erased;
>
> d EU citizens and enterprises are granted the same defence rights and procedural guarantees and the same right of access to justice as exist in the EU and that the legality and proportionality of the transfer requests are open to judicial review in the US;
>
> e transferred data are subject to the same judicial redress mechanisms as would apply to data held within the EU, including compensation in the event of unlawful processing of personal data; and
>
> f the agreement prohibits any use of SWIFT data by US authorities for purposes other than those linked to terrorism financing, and that the transfer of such data to third parties other than the public authorities in charge of the fight against terrorism financing is also prohibited.
>
> (European Parliament 2009b)

The Parliament's resolution also demanded that data concerning transactions relating to the Single European Payment Area (SEPA), where payments are made and received in euro, should fall outside the scope of the data to be requested by or transferred to the Treasury Department.

Proportionality Principle

It should be noted that, in adopting the resolution, the European Parliament did not look for a wholesale ban on the transfer of financial data originating from the EU for the purpose of the TFTP. Rather it was concerned with the need to "strike the right balance between security measures and the protection of civil liberties and fundamental rights, while ensuring the utmost respect for privacy and data protection" (European Parliament 2009b, 1).

In this connection, it deserves mention that the Parliament, drawing on the expert opinion of the European data protection authorities, advocated the proportionality principle in its resolution. As noted, the Parliament insisted that the processing of financial transaction should not be disproportionate to the objective for which such data would have been transferred and subsequently processed. The Parliament also maintained that SWIFT data transfer should only be sent by a "push" system—that is, data should be sent ("pushed") by Europeans rather than accessed ("pulled") by US authorities. With a "push" system, EU authorities could conceivably control the transfer of data so that they would be "adequate, relevant and not excessive" in relation to the purposes for which they are further processed. To "push" data, however, the EU needed to have its own data processing system. The Parliament's resolution thus suggested that "it may be useful for the [European] Commission to evaluate the necessity of setting up a European TFTP" (European Parliament 2009b, 12).

TFTP I

In July 2009, the European Council approved the beginning of negotiations with the US government for an agreement on the transfer of SWIFT data,

> knowing that in the absence of such … agreement an important security gap would arise in which there would be a risk of losing the benefit of important leads obtained through the Terrorist Finance Tracking Programme [*sic*] from European financial transactions for future terrorism investigations.
>
> (Council of European Union 2010a, p. 1)

On November 30, 2009, the Council Presidency and the Department of Homeland Security agreed on a legal framework for the transfer of financial transactions data from the jurisdiction of the EU to the US for the purposes of the TFTP. The agreement (commonly called TFTP I or SWIFT I) was then referred to the European Parliament for its necessary approval under the Lisbon Treaty, which had entered into force on December 1, 2009.[7]

The TFTP agreement (also known as the SWIFT agreement), by and large, was a legally binding version of the representations that the Treasury Department gave in June 2007. The agreement, in fact, had similar provisions as US representations regarding limitation of purpose, prohibition of data mining, security, data retention and deletion as well as data subjects' right to seek redress in case of a breach of the agreement. At the same time, the agreement did include new provisions on joint review of the implementation of the agreement and "cooperation with future equivalent EU system" on the basis of reciprocity.[8] According to the European Council, the agreement contained "an important number of the guarantees which were called for in the European Parliament's Resolution of 17 September 2009" (Council of the European Union 2010a, p. 2).

Amid intense debate, however, on February 11, 2010, the European Parliament withheld its consent to the TFTP agreement, "against appeals from the Commission and the EU Presidency, against significant pressure from several Member States and against an unprecedented direct lobbying from the US side" (Monar 2010, p. 143), on the grounds that the deal fell short of the minimum safeguard requirements for SWIFT-derived data set out in the Parliament's September 2009 resolution (European Parliament 2010).[9]

TFTP II

Returning to square one, the EU and the US resumed negotiation in May 2010 and hammered out a new agreement (TFTP II or SWIFT II) on June 28, 2010. Several weeks earlier, US vice president Joe Biden had addressed the European Parliament, saying that the TFTP "is essential to our security, as well as to yours" (White House 2010). Such attentiveness by the US government paid off. In part because European financial industry was unhappy with the standoff (Farrell and Newman 2015), the European Parliament in July approved TFTP II, which the European Commission claimed had "taken into account the key points of the European Parliament's resolution" (Malmström 2010). The agreement entered into effect on August 1, 2010.

Like its predecessor, TFTP II provides that:

- transferred data should be used exclusively for counter-terrorism purposes (Article 1 and 5)[10];
- US requests should be tailored as narrowly as possible to minimize the amount of data requested (Article 4);
- any form of data mining is prohibited (Article 5);
- transferred data should be held in a secure physical environment (Article 5);

- "non-extracted" data should be deleted not later than five years from the date of receipt (Article 6); and
- the EU and the US would jointly review the safeguards, controls, and reciprocity provisions set in the agreement (Article 13).

Furthermore, the new agreement has added provisions on US data requests. Under TFTP II, the US Treasury may not seek any data relating to the SEPA. Related to this provision, Europol, the EU's law enforcement agency, must verify whether Treasury's request for data is justified by counter-terrorism needs and complies with the rule that data transfer requests should be tailored as narrowly as possible before data are sent to the US.

In addition, data subjects' rights were strengthened under TFTP II. The new agreement provides that any person has the right of access to his or her personal data as well as the right to seek the rectification, erasure, or blocking of his or her personal data when the data are inaccurate or mishandled.

Perhaps most importantly, TFTP II holds out the eventual elimination of "bulk" data transfers with the introduction of an EU equivalent of the TFTP. While the possibility of a "future equivalent EU system" was mentioned rather vaguely in TFTP I, Article 11 of TFTP II explicitly states:

1 During the course of this Agreement, the European Commission will carry out a study into the possible introduction of an equivalent EU system allowing for a more targeted transfer of data.
2 If, following this study, the European Union decides to establish an EU system, the United States shall cooperate and provide assistance and advice to contribute to the effective establishment of such a system.

As noted, SWIFT data have until now been transferred in a large volume for the purpose of the TFTP and extracted *within the jurisdiction of the US*. Once an EU TFTP system comes into operation, however, financial messages will be sorted out *within the jurisdiction of the EU* and only those data relating to a specific terrorist track will be sent to the US (which will also ensure that data relating to transactions within the SEPA will be excluded in pursuant to a new provision of TFTP II). Setting up an EU TFTP would thus imply a more limited transfer of data to the US, helping ensure an "adequate, relevant and not-excessive" use of data on financial transactions originating from Europe in accordance with European data protection standards.

EU TFTS?

It has been observed that the European Parliament's involvement in the formal policy process was one of the "factors that have contributed to strengthening the EU's negotiation position" *vis-à-vis* the US (Quesada

Gámez and Mincheva 2012, p. 311). With TFTP II, the European Parliament is said to have "achieved inclusion of certain judicial safeguards and measures for citizen protection" (de Goede 2012a, p. 11)—most importantly, the introduction of an EU-managed data transfer system.

The elimination of "bulk" transfer indeed was the "key to the deal for the European Parliament" (European Parliament 2010). For many members of the European Parliament the promise of data analysis capacities on European soil through an EU equivalent of the TFTP was one of the preconditions for approving TFTP II (Wesseling 2014). However, work on setting up what subsequently was dubbed a European Terrorist Finance Tracking System (EU TFTS) had a false start.

When approving TFTP II, the European Council and the European Parliament invited the European Commission to submit, within one year of the date of entry into force of the agreement, "a legal and technical framework for extraction of data on EU territory" and to present, within three years of the date of entry into force of the agreement, a progress report on the "development of an equivalent EU system" (Council of the EU 2010b). In practice, this meant that the Commission was to submit "a legal and technical framework" before August 1, 2011, and a progress report before August 1, 2013.

In response, on July 13, 2011, the European Commission delivered the first communication to the Parliament and the Council on an EU TFTS (European Commission 2011). This communication described five available options for the establishment of a "legal and technical framework" for extraction of data on EU soil. In November 2013, the Commission published the second communication on an EU TFTS. The communication once again assessed possible options for an EU TFTS, taking into account the principles of necessity, proportionality, cost-effectiveness and respect for fundamental rights. The communication then concludes: "In light of the information gathered, the case to present at this stage a proposal for an EU TFTS is not clearly demonstrated" (European Commission 2013a, p. 14). In other words, the European Commission suggested that the status quo might be a reasonable course of action to take. The Commission argues that

> in order to extract data on EU soil it would be necessary to create and manage a new database containing all the information of EU citizens' financial transfers.
>
> The creation of such database would raise serious challenges in term of data storage, access and protection, not to mention the huge technical and financial efforts that would be needed. Any EU system would be data intrusive and would therefore require robust data protection guarantees and safeguards to be put in place. It would be costly and also technically and operationally demanding to set up and maintain.
>
> (European Commission 2013d)

After the Deluge

The controversy over the transfers of data, including financial transaction data, to the US was renewed in 2013 with the media reports on mass electronic surveillance activities by US National Security Agency (NSA) (see chapters 4 and 5).

The European Parliament reacted harshly to the media reports. On July 4, 2013, the European Parliament adopted a resolution that expressed serious concern over PRISM and other such programs that "entail a serious violation of the fundamental right of EU citizens and residents to privacy and data protection" and suggested the possible suspension of the PNR and TFTP agreements with the US (European Parliament 2013a)[11].

The European Parliament made a more strongly worded appeal for the suspension of the TFTP agreement in its resolution of October 23, 2013, which was adopted in response to press reports since September 2013 that the NSA had direct access to financial payment messages referring to financial transfers and related data held by SWIFT (European Parliament 2013b).

The European Commission, however, expressed its belief that the NSA had not had access to SWIFT data outside the scope of the EU–US agreement as the Commission had received a written assurance that the US government had not breached the TFTP agreement and would continue to respect it fully (European Commission 2013c).[12] The European Parliament was not convinced and, in its resolution of March 12, 2014, once again asked the Commission for the suspension of the TFTP agreement. The Parliament took the view that

> the information provided by the European Commission and the US Treasury does not clarify whether US intelligence agencies have access to SWIFT financial messages in the EU by intercepting SWIFT networks or banks' operating systems or communication networks, alone or in cooperation with EU national intelligence agencies and without having recourse to existing bilateral channels for mutual legal assistance and judicial cooperation …
>
> (European Parliament 2014, 53)

Although the European Parliament has no formal power to initiate the suspension or termination of an international agreement, it was expected that the Commission would have to act if the Parliament withdrew its support for the TFTP agreement (European Parliament 2013b). It remains to be seen what impact the European Parliament—with its newly acquired power under the Lisbon Treaty—can have on the future of the TFTP agreement.

Conclusion

While part of the tendency to "make more and not less personal data available to law enforcement authorities" (Den Boer and Monar 2002, p.

27), the TFTP agreement reflects the EU's effort to make the processing of private financial data originating from the EU consistent with the European data protection regime. Given that the US TFTP was launched at a time of a national emergency, it was remarkable that the EU gained the concession from the US that it would restrict the use of data potentially of great value in combating terrorist financing.

It should be emphasized that, like the PNR case, the core of controversy in the SWIFT affair was not *whether* personal data should be deployed for security purposes, but *how* personal data should be used for such purposes. As with the PNR talks, therefore, the EU–US negotiations over financial data revolved around the issue of establishing a legal framework for data transfer that would ensure that European standards of protection would be met within the US jurisdiction.

Importantly, the EU agreed to make financial transaction data originating in the EU available to US authorities, but not at the expense of the integrity of the EU data privacy regime. Rather, the EU negotiated with the US for an agreement that would proscribe "disproportionate and excessive" use of personal data originating from the EU by US authorities. The EU has also sought to preclude the need to transfer "disproportionate" amounts of data and established a prospect of bringing transfer operations within the purview of European authorities. In other words, by attempting to shift the locus of the analytical and filtering process, the EU tried to (re)gain control over personal data originating within its jurisdiction.

Like the PNR dispute, the SWIFT affair is an example of a growing tendency to use information held in the private sector for public security purposes (Klosek 2007). Private entities now hold a vast amount of data that may be valuable for law enforcement or intelligence activities. The SWIFT affair illustrates the difficulty of balancing security interests against privacy concerns, which are generally respected but might be dismissed under extreme circumstances.

Notes

1 For instance, in 2005, SWIFT delivered 10 million messages a day on average to over 7800 financial institutions in 204 countries and territories (SWIFT Annual Report 2005).
2 IEEPA authorizes the president, during a declared national emergency, to investigate bank transfers and other transactions in which a foreign person has any interest.
3 UNPA authorizes the president, when implementing United Nations (UN) Security Council Resolutions, to investigate economic relations or means of communication between any foreign person and the US.
4 It should be noted that SWIFT is subject to the Belgian data protection law that implements the EU Data Protection Directive because the co-operative has its headquarters in Belgium.
5 de Goede (2012a) points out that these controls and safeguards consisted largely of the formalization of the privacy assurance that had been negotiated between SWIFT and the Treasury Department.

6 In early 2008 the European Commission designated the French counterterrorism judge Jean-Louis Bruguière for this purpose. In a report of December 2008, he confirmed the accuracy of the US Treasury Department's representations to the EU with respect to data protection practices and concluded that the TFTP had generated significant security benefits for the EU (General Secretariat of the Council of the EU 2009).

7 The TFTP agreement originally was intended to be transitional and applicable only for the short term so that it would be renegotiated under Lisbon Treaty rules.

8 Article 9 provides that "[i]n the event that an EU system equivalent to the US TFTP is implemented in the European Union or in one or more of its Member States that requires financial payment messaging data stored in the United States to be made available in the European Union, the US Treasury Department shall actively pursue, on the basis of reciprocity and appropriate safeguards, the cooperation of any relevant international financial payment messaging service providers which are based in the territory of the United States."

9 It should be noted that, unlike the PNR case, the Parliament did not have to worry about the need for an EU–US agreement for a common legal basis because the SWIFT accord would cover data held by only one company—that is, SWIFT.

10 It should be recalled that the European Parliament had expressed concern that the transfer of information on economic activities could give rise to large-scale forms of economic and industrial espionage.

11 Article 21 of the TFTP agreement provides that "Either Party may suspend the application of this Agreement with immediate effect, in the event of breach of the other Party's obligations under this Agreement."

12 Cecilia Malmström, then European Commissioner for Home Affairs, and David Cohen, Under-Secretary of the US Department of the Treasury for Terrorism and Financial Intelligence exchanged letters in September 2013, following the press reports.

8 Data Privacy and Free Trade Agreements

Data privacy remains a contentious issue in the transatlantic relationship. In addition to the cases analyzed in the previous chapters, data protection has indeed been heatedly discussed in relation to the negotiations between the European Union (EU) and the United States (US) on the proposed Transatlantic Trade and Investment Partnership (TTIP) agreement.

While past free trade agreements (FTAs) mainly dealt with tariffs, recent FTAs tend to be broader in scope, often covering "new issues" such as intellectual property rights, investment, trade in services, and regulatory cooperation. From the viewpoint of data privacy, FTAs might pose a challenge when they contain a provision to facilitate free flows of data or prohibit legal or regulatory measures that would impede data flows among parties. It should be recalled that data protection at the international level entails some kinds of restrictions on the movement of personal data across borders. Depending on perspectives, such restrictions might be seen as barriers to cross-border flows of data and, by extension, non-tariff barriers to trade—particularly trade in digital services and electronic commerce (e-commerce). It is in this context that data protection and privacy have intertwined in FTAs, such as TTIP, the Trans-Pacific Partnership (TPP) agreement, and the Trade in Services Agreement (TiSA).

Data Privacy and FTAs

Proliferation of FTAs has been a salient feature of the global economy in recent years. FTAs are not a new phenomenon. Nonetheless, the number of regional trade agreements (RTAs (i.e. FTAs and customs unions)) notified to the General Agreement on Tariffs and Trade (GATT) remained low until the 1980s. Since the 1990s, however, the GATT and its successor, the World Trade Organization (WTO), have been notified of a substantially larger number of RTAs. As a result, the cumulative number of notified RTAs has rapidly increased. By 2016, more than 400 RTAs cumulatively had been notified to the GATT/WTO.[1]

Countries have increasingly turned to trade agreements on a bilateral or regional basis, foremost because they are frustrated with the slow (or rather lack of) progress in the multilateral trade negotiations ("rounds") held by the WTO. Compared with the rounds of the WTO, which has 164 members,[2] FTA negotiations usually involve a much smaller number of parties and, thus, tend to be less complicated as well as more flexible. This relative simplicity and flexibility, in turn, often allows FTAs to cover "new issues" on which global (i.e. WTO) rules have not yet been established. Free flow of data is one of these "new issues."

From the perspective of economic interests, cross-border flow of data, including personal data, is a vital part of business operations in the digitalized world. To repeat a point made previously, however, transnational data protection might necessitate some kinds of restrictions on the use and transfer of personal data across borders. For example, data export limitation—as provided by Article 45 of the EU General Data Protection Regulation and Article 25 of the EU Data Protection Directive—effectively restrict flows of personal data to a foreign jurisdiction.

As such, from the economic perspective, certain data protection measures might be seen as barriers to cross-border flows of data and, therefore, barriers to international trade, especially trade in sectors that heavily rely on data (e.g. financial services and electronic commerce). So FTAs that seek to promote digital trade may prohibit data protection measures that impede free flows of data.

From the perspective of privacy, however, there is a concern that FTAs "may act as limitations on the operation of privacy law" (Greenleaf 2016, p. 2). Theoretically, if there is no barrier to cross-border data flows, personal data might be processed in a country where data protection standards are lower than the country the data originate in. Thus, while some regulatory measures might be disguised trade barriers that are used to protect the domestic information industry or for other purposes unrelated to privacy, it is generally legitimate and justifiable—from the viewpoint of privacy—to regulate the use and transfer of data across borders. Such a pro-privacy argument leads to the claim that rules on cross-border data flows and data protection should be excluded from FTAs in order to protect individuals' right to privacy.

TTIP Negotiations

TTIP is a "comprehensive and high-standard" trade (and investment) liberalization agreement negotiated between the EU and the US (Akhtar and Jones 2014). The first round of TTIP negotiations was held in July 2013,[3] and 15 rounds of negotiations had been held by October 2016 (European Commission 2017).

TTIP negotiations cover a wide range of issues, including market access for goods and services, regulatory provisions that may serve as non-tariff barriers, as well as trade-related rules concerning intellectual property rights, public procurement, competition, state-owned enterprises, and the environment (Akhtar and Jones 2014; Puccio 2016). It should be noted that many issues dealt with in TTIP negotiations have not been addressed by the WTO.

If successfully concluded, this mega-regional free trade deal would cover more than 40 percent of global gross domestic product (GDP) and account for a large share of world trade (Akhtar and Jones 2014). By virtue of the sheer size of the transatlantic economy, the EU–US FTA could have significant influence on the future development of the rules and standards of the global trading system.

Data Privacy Issues in TTIP negotiations: US Stance

When TTIP was proposed, the issue of cross-border data flows was expected to be high on the negotiation agenda, because the US was interested in facilitating the movement of data across borders in a bid to promote digital services and electronic commerce (Akhtar and Jones 2014).[4] Facilitation of digital services and cross-border data flows, in fact, is one of the main US negotiating objectives described in the 2015 US Trade Promotion Authority (TPA) Act,[5] which allows the use of "fast-track authority" for TTIP and TPP (Puccio 2016). In the words of TPA, US principal negotiating objectives with respect to digital trade in goods and services, as well as cross-border data flows, are "to ensure that governments refrain from implementing trade-related measures that impede digital trade in goods and services, restrict cross-border data flows, or require local storage or processing of data."[6]

Implicit in these negotiating objectives is an assumption that, technically, whatever measures "restrict cross-border data flows" are non-tariff barriers to trade in the digital environment. This is at loggerheads with the data protection policy of the EU. "Local storage or processing of data" provides an illustrative example. While European data protection authorities think that the storage of relevant personal data on EU territory is an effective way to facilitate the exercise of control by data protection authorities and to ensure compliance with EU data protection requirements (Article 29 Working Party 2014b), the US government regards "requirements to provide services using local facilities or infrastructure" as a type of "localization barrier to trade," i.e. as a measure designed to protect, favor, or stimulate domestic industries, service providers, and/or intellectual property at the expense of goods, services, or intellectual property from other countries.[7] Because such measures can serve as "disguised trade barriers," claims the Office of the US Trade Representative (USTR), "it has been longstanding U.S. trade policy to advocate strongly against localization barriers."[8]

As noted, TPA explicitly states that the US negotiating objectives include a prohibition of requirement for "local storage or processing of data." According to the US Department of Commerce,

> The digital economy offers great opportunity, but challenges too ... . Governments around the world are increasingly pursuing protectionist

> policies that could restrict the free flow of information on the Internet. These rules, such as data localization requirements, present significant risks to the competitiveness of U.S. firms globally.[9]

Behind the stance of the US government on the issue of cross-border data flows are lobbying efforts of US industry that has interests in digital trade and electronic commerce. As the internet expands as a business platform, promotion of cross-border data flows has become a priority for US industry. In 2014, the US exported nearly $400 billion in digitally deliverable service, accounting for more than half of US service exports. Furthermore, the US is the largest producer of digital content that internet users consume worldwide (Fergusson and Williams 2016).

With regard to data flows across the Atlantic, US firms were concerned that, as the revelation of the National Security Agency (NSA) mass surveillance activity since June 2013 heightened Europeans' concern for data privacy, Europe might demand restrictions on cross-border data flows and, more specifically, require that servers be located in the EU for data privacy reasons (Akhtar and Jones 2014). The rationale behind such "data localization" is that, because personal data cannot be protected against US agencies once data are located on US servers, it is reasonable to require that some categories of data be stored and processed on local servers (Greenleaf 2016).

US industry's concern with the restrictions on cross-border data flows and "forced" localization barriers is clearly expressed in the "policy priorities" document released by the National Foreign Trade Council (NFTC) in November 2011.[10] Titled "Promoting Cross-Border Data Flows: Priority for the Business Community," the document maintains that "explicit prohibition of restrictions on legitimate cross-border information flows and prohibition of local infrastructure or investment mandates" should be included in the objectives that the US government seeks in international commitments.[11] In the "policy priorities" document, US companies, including Citi, Google, IBM, Mastercard, Microsoft, and Visa, as well as associations such as Business Software Alliance, Coalition of Services Industries, Software & Information Industry Association, and US Council for International Business, argue as follows:

> A variety of countries have introduced or enacted measures that would compel financial services providers to process data on-shore or require online service providers or other companies to locate physical infrastructure such as servers within their borders … . [Such] measures are both discriminatory and contrary to the notion of cross-border trade. Governments should commit to prohibit measures that would require service providers to locate infrastructure within a country's borders or operate locally.[12]

Likewise, the Business Coalition for Transatlantic Trade, founded by the US Chamber of Commerce, argues as follows:

> It [TTIP] should include commitments to foster cross-border flows of information and access to digital products and services regardless of their method of delivery, and to prohibit requirements that service suppliers use local servers or other infrastructure or establish a local presence.[13]

More broadly, dissatisfied with the strict data protection standards of the EU, US industry has pressured for "interoperability" of EU and US data privacy rules. In this context, "interoperability" essentially means that US companies would be allowed to operate under the US data privacy rules when processing data originating in the EU (Fontanella-Khan 2013). Importantly, if EU and US data privacy rules become "interoperable," the transfer of personal data from the EU to the US would be brought out of the scope of the EU data protection rules on third-country transfers.

Data Privacy Issues in TTIP Negotiations: EU's Stance

The EU, on the other hand, was concerned that measures agreed upon as part of TTIP could undermine EU data protection standards. As noted, the NSA scandal heightened Europeans' concern for data privacy, elevating the prominence of data privacy issues in the TTIP negotiations (Akhtar and Jones 2014).

European data protection authorities were wary of the potential effect of TTIP on privacy. The European Data Protection Supervisor (EDPS) (2014), for example, released an opinion in February 2014, calling on the European Commission to ensure that "issues that might be negotiated under the TTIP, such as 'trans-border data flows', standards and certificates for the cloud or data security requirements do not have a negative impact on the protection of personal data." The Article 29 Working Party (2014b) also issued a statement in November 2014, saying that "[t]he European level of protection of personal data should not be eroded, wholly or in part, by bilateral or international agreements, including agreements on trade in goods or services with third countries."

Civil society groups have also raised objections against the inclusion of data protection in the TTIP talks. European Digital Rights (EDRi) claims that "[n]o provisions on data should be included in this [TTIP] deal" and that "trade negotiations are not an appropriate forum to discuss measures for the protection of privacy nor a place where to establish new standards" (EDRi 2015). Likewise, consumer organizations are concerned with the privacy implication of TTIP. The European Consumer Organisation (BEUC) has stated that it "is concerned that including data flows will result in a significant weakening of consumers' fundamental rights to privacy and to the protection of personal data."[14]

The European Commission, for its part, maintains that "[d]ata protection standards won't be part of the TTIP negotiations" and that "TTIP will make sure that the EU's data protection laws prevail over any commitments."[15] In the words of then justice commissioner Viviane Reding,[16]

> There are challenges to get it [TTIP] done and there are issues that will easily derail it. One such issue is data and the protection of personal data … . I warn against bringing data protection to the trade talks. Data protection is not red tape or a tariff. It is a fundamental right and as such it is not negotiable.
>
> (Fleming 2013)

The Council has endorsed the European Commission's policy to exclude data protection from the TTIP negotiations. In the meeting of November 2015, the Council of the EU debated the issue and concluded as follows:

> The Council stresses the need to create a global level playing field in the area of digital trade and strongly supports the Commission's intention to pursue this goal in full compliance with and without prejudice to the EU's data protection and data privacy rules, which are not negotiated in or affected by trade agreements.
>
> (Council of the EU 2015a)

In short, the EU refused to include data protection issues in TTIP negotiations. As a consequence, discussions on cross-border data flows were suspended (Puccio 2016).

The European Parliament, however, wants more than the mere exclusion of data protection issues from the TTIP negotiations. In July 2015, the European Parliament adopted a resolution that made recommendations on the TTIP negotiations to the European Commission. The resolution called on the European Commission, among other things,

> to ensure that the EU's acquis on data privacy is not compromised through the liberalisation of data flows ... [and] to incorporate ... a comprehensive and unambiguous horizontal self-standing provision ... that fully exempts the existing and future EU legal framework for the protection of personal data from the agreement ...
>
> (European Parliament 2015a, xii)

Furthermore, the resolution warned as follows:

> the consent of the European Parliament to the final TTIP agreement could be endangered as long as the US blanket mass surveillance activities are not completely abandoned and an adequate solution is found for the data privacy rights of EU citizens, including administrative and judicial redress.
>
> (European Parliament 2015a, xiii)

In other words, the European Parliament not only demanded a provision that would exclude data protection from TTIP but also linked its consent to

TTIP to the dismantling of US mass surveillance programs and the introduction of a proper redress mechanism for EU citizens (Puccio 2016).

TTIP and GATS

It should be noted that the exclusion of data protection from the TTIP negotiations is consistent with the general exception clauses of the WTO's General Agreement on Trade in Services (GATS), which entered into force in January 1995.[17] While the WTO has never decided on privacy—there is no such thing as a trade-related privacy agreement—it does address the issue in the context of trade in services.

Specifically, Article XIV of the GATS, which overrides all other provisions of the agreement, allows governments to adopt or enforce measures "necessary" to secure compliance with laws or regulations relating to "the protection of the privacy of individuals in relation to the processing and dissemination of personal data and the protection of confidentiality of individual records and accounts" (GATS Article XIV(c)(ii)). In other words, the GATS explicitly excludes data protection and privacy from its obligations, confirming that the provisions of the GATS do not limit data protection measures. However, such measures should not be applied in a manner that would constitute "unjustifiable discrimination between countries" or "disguised restriction on trade in services" (GATS Article XIV).

The GATS, along with other WTO agreements, constitutes a baseline for FTAs between WTO members. Indeed, the negotiation mandate for the European Commission refers to GATS Article XIV as follows: "[t]he Agreement will not preclude the enforcement of exceptions on the supply of services justifiable under the relevant WTO rules (Articles XIV and XIVbis GATS)" (Council of the EU 2013, point 17). It should be also noted that the "horizontal self-standing provision" that the European Parliament demanded is based on Article XIV of the GATS.

Death Knell for TTIP?

Currently, the TTIP negotiations are in a deep freeze (Blenkinsop 2016). The negotiations bogged down as the EU and the US could not reconcile their differences. It was said that the TTIP negotiations had failed,[18] even before the election to the US presidency of Donald Trump, who is hostile to international trade agreements.

While data protection has only partly contributed to the impasse of the TTIP talks, it is one of the most controversial issues in the negotiations of an agreement that is heavily criticized as potentially infringing on consumers' and citizens' rights in favor of corporations (Borger 2016).[19] The suspension of the discussion on data flows in the TTIP negotiations suggests that reaching an agreement is an arduous and highly difficult task between jurisdictions with different regulations and laws, and, by implication, different values and beliefs.

FTAs as a Vehicle to Promote EU Data Privacy Standards

The experience of the TTIP negotiations suggests that an FTA with a third country may pose a challenge to the EU's data protection regime. At the same time, however, an FTA with a third country might provide the EU an opportunity to promote the European notion that data privacy is a fundamental right. The FTA between the EU and South Korea illustrates this point.

The EU–South Korea FTA, the first trade deal the EU struck with an Asian country, was signed in October 2010 and took effect in 2011 (Council of the EU 2016a). While covering a variety of trade-related issues, the FTA provides as follows: "[e]ach Party, reaffirming its commitment to protect fundamental rights and freedom of individuals, shall adopt adequate safeguards to the protection of privacy, in particular with regard to the transfer of personal data" (Article 7.43).

In other words, the EU–South Korea FTA has a horizontal provision that requires, rather than permits, the parties to adopt data protection and privacy safeguards. However, it remains to be seen whether the EU–South Korea FTA will be a model for future FTAs between the EU and third countries. While some countries may be willing to include data privacy clauses in the agreement, others may be reluctant to do so and would prefer to include a clause that prohibits restrictions on data flows.

TPP Negotiations

TPP is a "comprehensive and high-standard" FTA among 12 countries in the Asia-Pacific region: Australia, Brunei, Canada, Chile, Japan, Malaysia, Mexico, New Zealand, Peru, Singapore, the US, and Vietnam. It should be noted that all TPP participants are also members of the Asia-Pacific Economic Cooperation (APEC) forum.[20] After these countries reached agreement on October 5, 2015, in Atlanta, TPP was signed on February 4, 2016, in Auckland (Fergusson and Williams 2016; Greenleaf 2016).

The evolution of the TPP grouping is rather complicated. The precursor of TPP is the Trans-Pacific Strategic Economic Partnership, which was concluded in 2006 by Singapore, New Zealand, Chile, and Brunei. This regional agreement among relatively small countries became a template for a mega-FTA covering the Pacific Rim when the US decided to negotiate with these four countries in 2008. Australia, Peru, and Vietnam also became negotiating partners that year. Malaysia became a negotiating partner of the renamed Trans-Pacific Partnership in 2010. Canada and Mexico entered into the TPP negotiations in 2012, followed by Japan in 2013 (Fergusson and Williams 2016).[21]

Like TTIP, TPP covers a wide range of issues. In addition to eliminating tariffs and non-tariff barriers to trade in goods, services, and agriculture, TPP as a twenty-first-century agreement is intended to establish or expand rules on trade-related issues, ranging from intellectual property rights to foreign direct investment to electronic commerce.

Also like TTIP, TPP is a mega-FTA. If implemented, TPP will cover roughly 40 percent of global GDP. TPP, indeed, will be the world's largest plurilateral FTA by value of trade (Fergusson and Williams 2016). Accordingly, the rules and standards codified in TPP are likely to have significant impact on the global trading system.

Data Privacy Issues in TPP

TPP is the first multilateral trade agreement with detailed provisions relating to privacy protection. Regional FTAs, or bilateral FTAs, completed prior to the signature of TPP in 2016, have rarely included privacy-related clauses (Greenleaf 2016).

The most important privacy-related provisions of TPP are stipulated in chapter 14 ("Electronic Commerce"), which applies to "measures adopted or maintained by a Party that affect trade by electronic means" (Article 14.2.2).[22] Overall, this chapter has been written with the recognition that "frameworks that promote consumer confidence in electronic commerce" are important and that "unnecessary barriers to its use and development" should be avoided (Article 14.2.1).

One of the key provisions of chapter 14 is Article 14.8 ("Personal Information Protection"), which requires that "each Party shall adopt or maintain a legal framework that provides for the protection of the personal information of the users of electronic commerce." It should be noted that this requirement is made for the purpose of "enhancing consumer confidence in electronic commerce" (TPP Article 14.8.1). In other words, privacy in TPP is conceived as protection of consumers' rights rather than of basic human rights. This conception is consistent with the overall aim of the chapter to promote digital trade and electronic commerce.

Another key provision of chapter 14 is Article 14.11, which addresses "Cross-Border Transfer of Information by Electronic Means." While recognizing that "each Party may have its own regulatory requirements concerning the transfer of information by electronic means" (Article 14.11.1), the article provides that "each Party shall allow the cross-border transfer of information by electronic means, including personal information" (Article 14.11.2). This means that, in principle, national measures that restrict cross-border information flows are prohibited.

This general prohibition of restrictions on cross-border data flows is reinforced by the prevention of data localization requirement specified in Article 14.13, which addresses "Location of Computing Facilities" (i.e. computer servers and storage devices for processing or storing information for commercial use). While recognizing that "[e]ach Party may have its own regulatory requirements regarding the use of computing facilities, including requirements that seek to ensure the security and confidentiality of communications" (Article 14.13.1), the article provides that "[n]o Party shall require a covered person to use or locate computing facilities in that

Party's territory as a condition for conducting business in that territory" (Article 14.13.2).

In sum, TPP's chapter on electronic commerce prohibits restrictions on cross-border data flows in general and data localization requirements in particular. In this way, according to the USTR, "TPP combats restrictions on cross-border data flows, data localization requirements, and other barriers to digital trade with cutting-edge obligations designed to promote the digital economy."[23] It should be noted that facilitation of cross-border data flows was among the US negotiating objectives laid out in the 2015 TPA Act, which allowed then president Barack Obama to close out negotiations on TPP. It should be also noted that US industry has called for free flows of data across borders to promote digital trade and electronic commerce.[24]

While both Article 14.11 and Article 14.13 provide for exceptions, it would be hard for governments to meet the criteria of the provisions (Greenleaf 2016).[25] To restrict cross-border data flows, governments have to show that the restriction is legitimate, non-discriminatory, and proportionate. Thus, critics claim that TPP would deprive governments of the "rights to regulate" cross-border data flows. According to the Electronic Frontier Foundation (EFF), TPP places barriers in the way of protecting privacy as it outlaws strong privacy laws if they amount to an "arbitrary or unjustifiable discrimination or a disguised restriction on trade."[26]

TPP at Dead End?

The prospects for TPP are bleak. The agreement has been signed, but it is highly uncertain whether TPP will come into force.

There are two ways by which TPP may come into force. It can enter into effect 60 days after the twelfth ratification by the original signatories in the first two years from its signature. In other words, it must be ratified by all parties to enter into force within two years. Thereafter, TPP may enter into effect if at least six signatory countries representing 85 percent of the bloc's 2013 GDP have ratified the agreement. This threshold is likely to require ratification by the two largest economies in the group, namely, the US and Japan (Fergusson and Williams 2016; Greenleaf 2016).

So the TPP deal was doomed when the US formally abandoned it. On January 23, 2017, US president Donald Trump, who had taken office three days before, signed an executive order to withdraw from TPP, former president Barack Obama's signature trade achievement (Baker 2017). The US's abandonment of TPP has made its entry into force difficult and is likely to discourage other parties from ratifying the agreement. For now, the revival of TPP is unlikely unless the Trump administration changes its policy on international trade agreements.

TiSA Negotiations

TiSA is a plurilateral agreement to liberalize trade in services. Currently, TiSA is negotiated by 23 members of the WTO (or 50 countries[27]), including the world's largest advanced economies such as the US, the EU, and Japan.[28] Together, the participating countries represent approximately 70 percent of the world's $55 trillion services market.

The negotiations on TiSA started formally in March 2013. By November 2016, 21 rounds of negotiations had been held. Intended to go beyond the GATS, the TiSA negotiations cover a broad array of sectors and issues. The negotiating parties discuss not only the areas that the GATS already covers—such as telecommunications, maritime transport, and financial services—but also "new" areas, including electronic commerce.[29]

TiSA and Data Protection

While negotiated by a group of like-minded countries outside the WTO round,[30] TiSA is based on the GATS, which involves all WTO members. This means that all negotiated provisions will be compatible with the GATS provisions on scope, definitions, disciplines related to market access and national treatment, as well as exceptions (European Commission 2016d).

This supposed compatibility of TiSA with the GATS has an important implication for data protection. As noted, Article XIV of the GATS provides that the protection of data privacy may be an exception to the obligations under the agreement. Thus, the European Commission affirms the following: "TiSA will contain the same safeguards for protecting data privacy that currently exist in the GATS. This means that countries can continue to apply their confidentiality and data protection laws" (European Commission 2016d, p. 9).

Based on such understanding, the EU has refrained from putting forward a proposal on cross-border data flows (Fefer 2017). This exclusion of data flows from TiSA negotiations is in line with the European Parliament's recommendations on TiSA negotiations. In a resolution of February 3, 2016, the Parliament recommended to the European Commission "to take a cautious approach to the negotiation of chapters concerning data and privacy protection" and "to ensure that European citizens' personal data flow globally in full compliance with the data protection and security rules in force in Europe" (European Parliament 2016e, 1(c)ii and iv).

TiSA and Cross-border Data Flows

From the US point of view, however, the EU's reluctance to engage in discussions on data flows has created an obstacle in the negotiations (Fefer 2016). The US stance, indeed, is very different from that of the EU. According to the USTR,

> TiSA will encompass state-of-the-art trade rules aimed at promoting fair and open trade across the full spectrum of service sectors—from telecommunications and technology to distribution and delivery services. TiSA will also take on new issues confronting the global marketplace, like restrictions on cross-border data flows that can disrupt the supply of services over the Internet …

Presumably, such a US government view has been influenced by the stance of US industry. The US Chamber of Commerce argues as follows:

> The TiSA should safeguard cross-border data flows. In today's global economy, companies often move data across borders to create new products, enhance productivity, deter fraud, protect consumers, and grow their business. Recent studies estimate that within ten years products and services reliant on cross-border data flows will add over $1 trillion annually to the global economy, with the United States at the fore.
>
> To seize these benefits, the TiSA should prohibit restrictions on legitimate cross-border information flows and bar local infrastructure mandates relating to data storage.[31]

Reportedly, the issue of "trade barriers to cross-border data flows" is likely to be addressed in an annex on electronic commerce, along with such issues as consumer online protection and interoperability (Fefer 2017). Specifically, the proposed electronic commerce annex is likely to contain provisions that prohibit restrictions on cross-border data transfers and data localization (EDRi 2016). Furthermore, the issue of cross-border data flows is likely to be covered in an annex on financial services, which may be carved out of the e-commerce annex. Specifically, the US has proposed language that would prohibit financial service regulators from imposing barriers to cross-border data flows and data localization requirements except in certain circumstances (Fefer 2017). Critics argue that these TiSA provisions would enable cross-border data transfers and data processing without adequate safeguards (EDRi 2016).

It is noteworthy that TiSA may include the issue of cross-border data flows in a very similar way to TPP. Thus, even if TPP has been abandoned, a ban on restrictions of cross-border data flows might revive in TiSA, setting a precedent for such provisions in future FTAs. However, the EU is set to maintain all existing EU and national laws on privacy protection, including those pertaining to financial services (Fefer 2017).

Conclusion

FTAs are likely to be among the defining factors in the future evolution of data protection and privacy laws (Greenleaf 2016). The experience of TTIP, TPP, and TiSA suggests that, while FTAs provide fora for promoting open access to digital goods, services, and information with willing trading partners, they may also interfere with participating states' "rights to regulate," including the "right" to restrict cross-border data flows for the purpose of data and privacy protection.

In the TTIP, TPP, and TiSA negotiations, one of the major objectives of the US has been the facilitation of free flows of data across borders. From the US perspective, which is closely aligned with US economic interests, data protection laws and regulation are relevant to international trade, because they might adversely affect cross-border flows of data, the lifeblood of the digital economy.

From the EU's perspective, on the other hand, international trade is relevant to data protection, because cross-border data flows might have negative impacts on privacy. To the EU, regulation of cross-border data flows is legitimate and necessary to protect EU citizens' right to privacy. Thus, the EU has insisted in the TTIP and TiSA talks that the issue of cross-border data flows should be excluded from the negotiations. Rather, the EU would like to include a data and privacy protection clause in the FTAs it participates in, as it did in the bilateral FTA with South Korea.

While TTIP and TPP have seemingly "failed," and TiSA is yet to be concluded, the US is likely to continue to pursue the objective of free flows of data in bilateral FTA negotiations with its trading partners. Similarly, the EU is likely to maintain its stance on the issues relating to data protection and privacy, seeking to promote the notion that privacy is a fundamental right. Through FTAs, therefore, the gap between the EU and the US over cross-border data flows and data protection is likely to be projected on to the global trading system. In short, the debate goes on.

Notes

1 World Trade Organization (WTO), Regional Trade Agreements: Facts and Figures, www.wto.org/english/tratop_e/region_e/regfac_e.htm, accessed March 29, 2017.

2 WTO, Members and Observers, www.wto.org/english/thewto_e/whatis_e/tif_e/org6_e.htm, accessed March 29, 2017.

3 On March 20, 2013, the Obama administration notified Congress of its intent to enter into TTIP negotiations (Akhtar and Jones 2014). For their part, on June 14, 2013, EU member states mandated the European Commission to start negotiations with the US and adopted guidelines for the European Commission (European Commission 2016h).

4 The Obama Administration's letter that notified Congress of the US intent to enter into negotiations with the EU contained specific objectives for negotiations in electronic commerce and communication technology services, including the development of appropriate provisions to facilitate the movement of cross-border data flows. Letter from Demetrios Marantis, Acting US Trade Representative, to John Boehner, Speaker, US House of Representatives, March 20, 2013, https://ustr.gov/sites/default/files/03202013%20TTIP%20Notification%20Letter.PDF, accessed November 11, 2016.

5 TPA defines US negotiating objectives and priorities for trade agreements and establishes consultation and notification requirements for the President to follow throughout the negotiation process. At the end of the negotiation and consultation process, Congress gives the agreement an up-or-down vote, without amendment. Office of the US Trade Representative, "Trade Promotion Authority," https://ustr.gov/trade-topics/trade-promotion-authority, accessed November 11, 2016.

6 S.995 – Bipartisan Congressional Trade Priorities and Accountability Act of 2015.

7 Other examples of localization barriers include local content requirements, i.e. requirements to purchase domestically manufactured goods or domestically supplied services; subsidies or other preferences that are only received if producers use local goods, locally owned service providers, or domestically owned or developed intellectual property, or intellectual property that is first registered in that country; measures to force the transfer of technology or intellectual property; requirements to comply with country- or region-specific or design-based standards that create unnecessary obstacles to trade; and unjustified requirements to conduct or carry out duplicative conformity assessment procedures in-country.

8 Office of the United States Trade Representative, "Localization Barriers to Trade," https://ustr.gov/trade-topics/localization-barriers, accessed March 22, 2016.

9 The International Trade Administration (ITA), US Department of Commerce, "Digital Attaché Program Information," www.export.gov/article?id=Digital-Attach%C3%A9-Program-Information, accessed March 22, 2016.

10 National Foreign Trade Council, "Promoting Cross- Border Data Flows: Priority for the Business Community," www.nftc.org/default/Innovation/PromotingCrossBorderDataFlowsNFTC.pdf, accessed March 22, 2016.

11 Other objectives include addressing emerging issues involving the regulation of the digital economy; promoting industry-driven international standards, dialogues, and best practices; and expanding trade in digital goods, services, and infrastructure.

12 National Foreign Trade Council, "NFTC, U.S. Business Community Leaders Roll Out Effort to Modernize Global Trade Rules on Cross-border Data Flows," press release, November 3, 2011, www.nftc.org/newsflash/newsflash.asp?Mode=View&id=236&articleid=3356&category=All, accessed March 22, 2016.

13 Business Coalition for Transatlantic Trade, Digital Trade, www.transatlantictrade.org/issues/digital-trade/, accessed March 29, 2017.

14 European Consumer Organisation (BEUC), "Data flows in TTIP," factsheet, www.beuc.eu/publications/beuc-x-2015-073_factsheet_data_flows_in_ttip.pdf, accessed December 2, 2016.

15 Fact sheet on services in TTIP, http://trade.ec.europa.eu/doclib/docs/2015/january/tradoc_152999.2%20Services.pdf, accessed October 20, 2016.

16 Reding made these comments in her speech at an event jointly arranged by Johns Hopkins University's School for Advanced International Studies and the EU's Washington DC mission.

17 WTO, "The General Agreement on Trade in Services (GATS): objectives, coverage and disciplines," www.wto.org/english/tratop_e/serv_e/gatsqa_e.htm, accessed April 10, 2017.

18 Then German economy minister Sigmar Gabriel reportedly said, "[t]he negotiations with the United States have de facto failed, even though nobody is really admitting it" (Farrell 2016).

19 The TTIP negotiations have been criticized not only by civil rights and consumer organizations but also by officials of major European countries. For

example, French trade minister Matthias Fekl called for an end to the TTIP negotiations because "[t]he Americans are giving us nothing" (Dalton 2016).

20 In fact, the framework for the TPP agreement was announced by then nine negotiating partners in November 2011 on the sidelines of the APEC ministerial meeting in Honolulu (Fergusson and Williams 2016).

21 Five more APEC member countries have stated that they wish to join the TPP: Indonesia, South Korea, Taiwan, Thailand, and the Philippines (Greenleaf 2016).

22 It should be noted that the scope of the measures that "affect" trade may be broader than measures that "govern" or "apply" to trade (Greenleaf 2016).

23 The Office of the United States Trade Representative (USTR), "Fact Sheet: Key Barriers to Digital Trade," https://ustr.gov/about-us/policy-offices/press-office/fact-sheets/2016/march/fact-sheet-key-barriers-digital-trade, accessed March 22, 2016.

24 For instance, in a statement titled "Promoting cross-border information and data flows in the TPP," Business Roundtable and other US business associations argued that "the TPP negotiations should produce legally binding commitments to [...] [p]ermit cross-border information and data flows" and "[p]rohibit requirements to use local computing infrastructure, such as servers, as a condition for doing business or investment in a TPP country or engaging in e-commerce or cross-border trade." Business Roundtable, "Statement: Promoting Cross-Border Information and Data Flows in the TPP," press release, July 2, 2012, http://businessroundtable.org/media/news-releases/statement-promoting-cross-border-information-and-data-flows-in-the-t, accessed April 7, 2017.

25 Article 14.11.3 allows for measures inconsistent with the prohibition of cross-border data flow restrictions to achieve a "legitimate public policy objective," if the measure is not applied discriminatorily or as a disguised trade restriction and is proportionate to the objective. Likewise, Article 14.13.3 allows for measures inconsistent with the prohibition of data location requirement to fulfill a "legitimate public policy objective," as long as the measure "is not applied in a manner which would constitute a means of arbitrary or unjustifiable discrimination or a disguised restriction on trade" and "does not impose restrictions on the use or location of computing facilities greater than are required to achieve the objective."

26 Electronic Frontier Foundation, "Trans-Pacific Partnership Agreement," www.eff.org/ja/issues/tpp, accessed April 7, 2017.

27 This means about one third of WTO member countries are now involved in TiSA.

28 Participants in the TiSA negotiations are Australia, Canada, Chile, Chinese Taipei, Colombia, Costa Rica, the EU, Hong Kong (China), Iceland, Israel, Japan, Korea, Liechtenstein, Mauritius, Mexico, New Zealand, Norway, Pakistan, Panama, Peru, Switzerland, Turkey, and the US.

29 European Commission, Trade in Services Agreement (TiSA), http://ec.europa.eu/trade/policy/in-focus/tisa/, accessed March 27, 2017; Office of the USTR, Trade in Services Agreement, https://ustr.gov/TiSA, accessed March 27, 2017.

30 TiSA talks, indeed, were launched by the "Really Good Friends of Services," a group of WTO members that were interested in liberalization of trade in services (Hufbauer and Cimino-Isaacs 2015).

31 US Chamber of Commerce, "Trade in Services Agreement," dated September 12, 2016, www.uschamber.com/issue-brief/trade-services-agreement, accessed March 29, 2017.

9 Conclusion

The politics of data has been an important but troublesome part of the transatlantic relationship. The European Union (EU) and the United States (US) have held rounds of negotiations and made a series of agreements on the transfer of commercial data, air passenger information, and financial transaction records. The EU–US negotiations and the resulting agreements on data transfer illustrate how the EU and the US have dealt with the problem of regulatory spillover or the extraterritorial reach of privacy and security regulation. In short, the cases represent the politics of extraterritoriality as well as the politics of data privacy.

Politics of Data Privacy

From the viewpoint of the politics of data privacy, the EU–US data talks represented the process through which a balance between privacy and other concerns, such as commercial interests and public security, was struck.

In the EU–US negotiations that led to the Safe Harbor arrangement, the question was not *whether* but *how* personal data should be transferred from the jurisdiction of the EU and subsequently used in the US. The EU and the US solved this question by agreeing on a set of rules and conditions upon which data could be transferred, including certain restrictions on the use of data by US companies. Recently, the Safe Harbor scheme has been replaced by the Privacy Shield, but this newly negotiated framework functions in a very similar way as its predecessor.

Likewise, in the passenger name record (PNR) and Society for Worldwide Interbank Financial Transactions (SWIFT) negotiations, the question once again was not *whether* but *how* data containing personal information should be transferred and used by the US government. While allowing the US government to access data originating in the EU, the PNR and Terrorist Financing Tracking Program (TFTP) agreements effectively restricted certain information practices by US authorities with regard to such data. Given the utility of personal data for counterterrorism and law enforcement, it is remarkable that the US agreed to limit, for example, the categories of data to be transferred, the purposes for which the transferred data were to be used, and the period of time to retain such data. The EU–US Umbrella Agreement on data protection is also noteworthy in this respect as it provides for similar safeguards.

In sum, the EU–US data negotiations sought to strike a balance between privacy on the one hand and commercial or security interests on the other by setting conditions and rules on the transfer and use of personal data. Generally speaking, however, the EU–US data agreements prioritize the flows of data between the transatlantic partners, which enjoy close economic and security relations.

Politics of Extraterritorial Regulation

From the perspective of the politics of extraterritorial regulation, the EU–US negotiations and agreements on data transfer exemplify the spillover effects of regulation across jurisdictions and responses to them. Specifically, they show how jurisdictions with different data privacy rules could cooperate to manage and facilitate the flows of data between them.

The Extraterritorial Reach of EU Regulation

The EU Data Protection Directive of 1995 was adopted in the context of the European project of creating a single market, but it had extraterritorial implications. Article 25 of the directive provides that transfer of personal data from EU territory to a third country (i.e. non-EU country) can take place only when the third country in question ensures an "adequate level of protection" of personal data. This extraterritorial provision essentially means that third countries need to meet EU data protection standards in order to receive personal data from the jurisdiction of the EU.

Unlike European countries, the US lacks a comprehensive privacy law that covers both public and private sectors. Thus, the US was deemed to fail to meet the adequacy requirement. If the Data Protection Directive was implemented to the letter, flows of personal data from the EU to the US could be disrupted.

US Response

Neither the US nor the EU wanted the disruption of transatlantic data flows. The US and the EU were each other's largest trading partners, and flows of personal data were an integral part of trade. To allow for continued flows of data, the US and the EU entered into negotiations, in which the US proposed a Safe Harbor arrangement. Under the arrangement, US organizations that self-declared to adhere to a set of privacy rules would be deemed to provide "adequate protection" and thus could import personal data from the jurisdiction of the EU without fear of being punished by European data protection authorities for violating the Data Protection Directive. In other words, the Safe Harbor arrangement provided a framework that would allow US companies to receive personal data from the EU, while complying with the requirements of the EU data protection law.

It is important to note that, under the Safe Harbor arrangement (and its successor, the Privacy Shield framework), the US did not enact new legislation, let alone a comprehensive privacy law. Rather, the US government agreed to sponsor a program that combined self-regulation of industry with the involvement of regulatory authority. In this sense, the Safe Harbor (and the Privacy Shield) essentially allowed the US to import data from the EU without making change to its legal regime or its policy that favored self-regulation. The US thereby refused to bear the cost of domestic adjustment.

The Extraterritorial Reach of US Regulation

Both the PNR dispute and the SWIFT affair stemmed from the extraterritorial reach of US counterterrorism regulations.

In the wake of the terrorist attacks of September 11, 2001, the US government began to collect and use PNR data to identify terrorists and deny their entry into the country. The requirement to submit PNR data was based on a domestic law of the US, but the measure had broad international ramifications as it was applied to all international passenger flights landing in the US. The Department of Homeland Security could impose such over-the-border obligations on non-US airlines by leveraging the authority to impose sanctions for noncompliance.

Around the same time, the US government began to use financial transaction data held by the SWIFT company for the purpose of the TFTP. Initially, the Treasury Department requested SWIFT's US operating center to turn over data on financial transactions that might be related to terrorist activities. However, the data held in SWIFT's server in the US contained information on not only transactions conducted inside the US but also transactions carried out *outside* the US. Thus, the request for SWIFT data had beyond-the-border implications. When SWIFT decided to change the architecture of its network, the US government sought to access the data held in SWIFT's server in Europe so that the TFTP would cover financial transactions worldwide.

It should be noted that in both the PNR and SWIFT cases, the US government intended to mitigate the negative effects that might arise from transactions with or in foreign jurisdictions. The requirement to submit PNR data was part of efforts to reduce risks associated with the cross-border movement of people. Likewise, the TFTP was established to manage adverse effects resulting from cross-border movement of money. In this sense, the PNR scheme and the TFTP can be seen as attempts to manage potentially negative effects arising from interdependence.

EU Response

In both the PNR and SWIFT cases, the EU adapted to the counter-terrorism measures of the US in the belief that information sharing was a vital part of transatlantic cooperation for counterterrorism. However, the EU did not simply subordinate itself to the measures the US unilaterally imposed. Rather, through negotiations, the EU as a "receptive state" sought to have the US policy fit into the European context. EU negotiators could leverage European data protection laws, most notably the Data Protection Directive, to gain concessions from the US.

The Department of Homeland Security's use of PNR data raised concerns in the EU, because PNR data contain personal information, possibly even sensitive information. If PNR data originating in the EU were misused in the US, then the privacy right of an EU citizen or resident would be infringed. Furthermore, if an EU data subject's right was infringed in the US, the effectiveness of the EU data protection regime would be compromised.

In legal terms, transfer of PNR data from the EU to the US was inconsistent with the Data Protection Directive since US laws were not deemed to provide adequate protection of the data relating to EU citizens. So the EU negotiated with the US for a framework for PNR transfer. The resulting PNR agreements of 2004, 2006, 2007, and 2012 set rules and conditions on the transfer and the subsequent use of PNR data originating in the EU. Significantly, these rules and conditions in effect restricted the US government's use of the PNR data originating in the EU so that the transfer and use of PNR data would be consistent with the EU data protection principles (e.g. processing of data should not be "disproportionate and excessive").

The use of SWIFT's data for the TFTP provoked controversy in the EU, because financial transaction data contain personally identifiable information. If financial transaction data originating in the EU were misused in the US, the privacy right of an EU citizen (and other users of SWIFT's services) would be infringed. Furthermore, had an EU data subject's right in the US been infringed, the efficacy of the EU data protection regime would have been undercut. So the EU negotiated with the US and gained assurances from the Treasury Department that the data originating in the EU would be handled adequately. Later, in response to the re-architecture of the SWIFT network, the EU and the US had another round of talks and reached the TFTP agreement of 2010. Notably, the TFTP agreement in effect limited the US authorities' use of SWIFT data so that the transfer and use of EU-originating financial transaction data would be consistent with the data protection rules of the EU.

In short, the EU, in both the PNR dispute and the SWIFT affair, sought to limit the potentially undermining effects of US counterterrorism measures on the integrity of the European data protection regime as well as the right of EU data subjects. Importantly, through negotiations with the US, the EU agreed to make EU-originating air passenger information and financial transactions data available to US authorities, but not without the pretense of compliance with its data protection regime.

Dual Role of the EU

The cases are highly complicated, partly because the EU assumed both receptive and assertive "state" roles in the course of negotiations with the US. As noted, in both the PNR and SWIFT cases the EU sought to shelter its data protection regime from the potentially negative impact of US counterterrorism regulations. This effort by the EU effectively resulted in the extraterritorial application of European privacy rules. For example, the EU insisted that processing of personal data should be proportionate and eventually gained concessions from the US that the data received from the EU would be limited in type and amount, used for limited purposes, and retained for a limited period of time. Given the priority placed on counterterrorism, it is remarkable that the PNR and SWIFT agreements led US law enforcement and intelligence authorities to make changes (or at least pledge to make changes) in their information practices that they would not have done otherwise.

Global Influence of the EU Data Protection Regulation?

The cases studied in this book suggest that the EU, to some extent, exerted influence over information practices of US businesses as well as US government authorities. If it were not for the agreements with the EU, US companies, the Department of Homeland Security, or the Treasury Department would have used personal data originating in the EU more extensively. In essence, the EU has insisted that European data should be protected in accordance with the European standards regardless of the location of the data.

Significantly, the EU's influence in data protection policy is not confined to the transatlantic relationship. Indeed, the EU is set to have *global* influence in this policy area. In the language of the "normative power Europe" thesis (Manners 2002), the EU's core norm of respect for human rights, including the right to privacy, could be diffused worldwide as the EU negotiates and concludes data transfer arrangements with other jurisdictions.

Currently, the EU is negotiating second-generation PNR agreements with a group of states that are interested in receiving air passenger data from the EU. Together with the first-generation agreements with the US, Canada, and Australia, future PNR accords might serve as a vehicle with which EU standards on the use of personal data for public security purposes spread across the globe. So might an agreement to share financial transaction data. At present, the EU only has the TFTP agreement with the US. However, similar agreements may be reached in the future with other third countries.

As for commercial data, Privacy Shield- or Safe Harbor-type agreements might provide the EU with venues to influence the information practices of third-country companies that have business in the EU market (which is large) and wish to have arrangements to streamline data transfer operations. To meet the adequacy requirement of the EU data protection law, such agreements would typically require third-country companies to accept certain conditions and rules on the processing of personal data imported from the jurisdiction of the EU. Since relatively few countries have been recognized by the European Commission as providing "adequate protection,"[1] there is a possibility that Privacy Shield- or Safe Harbor-type agreements between the EU and non-EU countries might be sought.

On a related note, free trade agreements with third countries might provide the EU an opportunity to promote the European notion that data privacy is a fundamental right. For example, the EU–South Korea Free Trade Agreement has a clause on data protection and privacy. Generally speaking, however, data protection provisions in FTAs between the EU and third countries have tended to be specific to sectors such as electronic commerce and financial services.[2]

The Extraterritorial Implication of the General Data Protection Regulation

Currently, the 1995 Data Protection Directive, the cornerstone of the EU data protection regime, is being replaced by the 2016 General Data Protection Regulation. Like the Data Protection Directive, the General Data Protection Regulation has clauses on the transfer of personal data to third countries. However, the extraterritorial implication of the regulation is not limited to the third-country transfer clauses. Significantly, the territorial scope of the regulation extends beyond the border of the EU in the sense that the regulation applies to any entity that processes data of EU data subjects regardless of the location of data-processing activities. Article 4.1 of the regulation provides as follows: "[t]his Regulation applies to the processing of personal data in the context of the activities of an establishment of a controller or a processor in the Union, regardless of whether the processing takes place in the Union or not."

Furthermore, a data controller or processor (i.e. firm) in a foreign jurisdiction is subject to the provisions of the General Data Protection Regulation so long as it engages in data-processing activities related to trade with EU data subjects or the monitoring of them. Article 4.2 of the regulation provides as follows:

> This Regulation applies to the processing of personal data of data subjects who are in the Union by a controller or processor not established in the Union, where the processing activities are related to:
>
> (a) the offering of goods or services, irrespective of whether a payment of the data subject is required, to such data subjects in the Union; or

(b) the monitoring of their behaviour as far as their behaviour takes place within the Union.

This extensive scope of application has serious implications for EU as well as non-EU companies that process data related to EU data subjects, because the regulation also provides for huge administrative fines. Specifically, the regulation provides that infringement of its provisions would lead to fines up to 20 million euros or up to 4 percent of the total worldwide annual turnover, whichever is higher (Article 83). For example, transfer of data to a third country that fails to meet the adequacy requirement will result in the imposition of such fines.

Significance of Territoriality

Perhaps paradoxically, the politics of extraterritoriality and counter-extraterritoriality in the PNR and SWIFT cases suggests that territoriality matters in the digitalized and interconnected world. It has been argued that the global diffusion of information communication technology has made territorial borders obsolete by allowing individuals and organizations to connect with each other directly regardless of geographical distances (Cairncross 1997; Spar and Bussgang 1996). However, detailed analyses of the PNR and SWIFT cases show that territoriality can be highly relevant to disputes that involve the information technology sector.

Territoriality and Extraterritoriality

To repeat a point made previously, the PNR disputes began with the beyond-the-border reach of US counterterrorism regulation. The US government could claim direct regulatory authority on non-US air carriers, because part of the activities of these transnational entities was conducted within US territory. It may be argued, therefore, that this US regulatory claim with broad extraterritorial implications was based on the territorial presence of foreign airlines.

Similarly, the SWIFT affair was set off by the beyond-the-border effects of US counterterrorism measures. The Treasury Department initially accessed SWIFT's data through SWIFT's US operation center. The US government could directly exert regulatory authority on SWIFT so long as part of the company's operations was carried out in US territory. SWIFT thus changed the network architecture so that EU-originating data would not be sent to its US operation center.

It should be noted that while data flow across jurisdictions, data operations are carried out in a specific place, which belongs to the territory of a specific state. As a principle of the Westphalian system, a sovereign state can exert authority over activities that have taken place within its territory. Thus, the US government could exercise regulatory authority over data held by entities that (at least partially) operate within the territorial jurisdiction of the US.

Territoriality and Counter-extraterritoriality

In both the PNR dispute and the SWIFT affairs, the EU sought to bring the crucial part of data transfer operations within its jurisdiction and thereby reduce the impact of the US claims of extraterritorial authority.

The latest PNR agreement, which was concluded in 2012, contains a provision whereby "carriers shall be required to transfer PNR to DHS [Department of Homeland Security] using the 'push' method" (Article 15). In other words, the agreement provides that PNR data should be sent ("pushed") by airlines rather than be accessed ("pulled") by US authorities. It is important to note that with a "push" system, PNR data transfer operations will be carried out *within the jurisdiction of the EU.* European authorities then will be able to ensure that only information on flights bound to the US be sent to the Department of Homeland Security. They also will be able to ensure that sensitive data be filtered out before data are sent to the US.

The TFTP agreement also seeks to shift the locus of data transfer operations. The 2010 TFTP agreement contains a provision related to an EU equivalent of US TFTP that might be established in the future. If an EU TFTP comes into existence, financial transaction data held in SWIFT's European operation centers will be sorted out *within the jurisdiction of the EU*, rather than extracted within the jurisdiction of the US. The Europeans then will be able to ensure that narrowly targeted data be sent to the US. In other words, the introduction of an EU TFTP would lead to the elimination of "bulk" data transfers pursuant to the proportionality principle (i.e. processing of personal data should be proportionate to the purpose for which the data are processed).

In summary, the EU has sought to (re)gain control over PNR and financial transaction data originating in Europe by altering the ways data are transferred. A switch to the "push" system and the establishment of the EU TFTP would preclude the need to transfer "disproportionate" amounts of data. Such measures would also bring data transfer operations within the purview of European data protection authorities to ensure compliance with EU data protection laws.[3]

Transborder Data Flows and Data Localization

The EU–US data disputes demonstrate the relevance of territoriality in the politics of data privacy. Territoriality, indeed, is a vital element of the ongoing politics of regulation concerning transborder data flows.

Data Localization

In principle, regulation, including data protection regulation, is enforced within a territorially defined jurisdiction. Logically, therefore, it would be easier to enforce data protection regulation, if data communication or storage equipment is located in the jurisdiction. Thus, efforts have been made at the national and regional levels to require or create incentives to localize data processing and storage.

Measures of data localization typically include rules that prevent data from being sent outside the territory. For example, Australia's Personally Controlled Electronic Health Records Act prohibits the transfer of health records outside the country. Another form of data localization consists of rules that require prior consent of the data subject before the data are transmitted across borders. For example, South Korea's Personal Information Protection Act requires information processors to inform and obtain consent from the individual for transferring personal information to a third party overseas. China's Information Security Technology Guidelines for Personal Information Protection with Public and Commercial Services Information System also prohibit the transfer of personal data abroad without express consent of the data subject or explicit regulatory approval. Yet another set of data localization rules requires data or copies of data to be stored domestically. For example, Russia's Federal Law No. 242 prohibits the storing of Russians' personal data outside the Russian Federation (Chander and Lê 2015).

Whatever the details of the provisions, these data localization requirements are intended to keep data within national or territorial borders. Since such requirements can be *de facto* barriers to transborder flows of data, opposition has been raised against data localization from the viewpoint of advancing free flows of data. Indeed, the Electronic Commerce Chapter of the Trans-Pacific Partnership (TPP) agreement prohibits signatory parties from requiring data localization.

An oft-cited rationale behind data localization is that personal data might not be protected adequately once the data are transferred outside the jurisdiction and hence the reach of national regulation. In other words, data localization has arguably been driven by concern about data privacy, which has grown in significance since the revelation of mass surveillance by US intelligence agencies.

However, there could be other motives for data localization. In some cases, data localization laws are rationalized on the grounds of national security and law enforcement. For example, Vietnam's Decree on Management, Provision, and Use of Internet Services and Information Content Online requires internet service providers to place at least a local server inside Vietnamese territory for law enforcement purposes (Chander and Lê 2015). In addition, there are cases in which national security and law enforcement are not explicitly stated but suspected purposes. For example, the aim of China's data transfer requirement is rather dubious, given the pervasive internet censorship in China (Deibert et al. 2011). Likewise, Russia's local storage requirement may possibly reflect the Russian government's desire to control electronic information flows.

Another possible, perhaps less insidious, motive behind data localization is the promotion of the national information technology industry. While data now are crucial raw materials of business activities, processing and storage of data has become a huge industry. To foster the domestic information technology industry, the government might "force" or create incentives to process and store data within the territory. In such a case, a data localization requirement can be seen as an industrial policy in disguise.

EU Data Protection Laws and Data Localization

Restrictions on transborder data flows are part of EU data protection laws. The Data Protection Directive provides that a transfer of personal data may take place only if the third country in question ensures an adequate level of data protection (Article 25). Likewise, the EU General Data Protection Regulation provides that a transfer of personal data to a third country or an international organization may only take place if the third country or an international organization in question ensures an adequate level of protection (Article 45) or if there are appropriate safeguards such as binding corporate rules, standard data protection clauses, and contractual clauses (Article 46).

It may be argued that these extraterritorial clauses of EU data protection laws constitute a localization barrier to transborder flows of data to the extent that they restrict the transfer of data to foreign jurisdictions. However, neither the Data Protection Directive nor the General Data Protection Regulation impose a total ban on the transfer of data; rather the laws set conditions under which personal data may be transferred to third countries. In other words, EU data protection laws permit transfer of data to a non-EU country so long as the country in question provides (what the EU deems) an adequate level of protection.

More controversial, perhaps, are recent talks in Europe about the possible development of a "virtual Schengen area," where digital data move freely between most EU and European Free Trade Association (EFTA) countries but not between the EU and third countries (e.g. the US).[4] The idea of creating a virtual external border for data dates back to 2011,[5] but it has gained considerable attention after the "Snowden revelation" of mass surveillance by US intelligence agencies (Kuner et al. 2015).

Closely related to the argument for the virtual Schengen area are the possibilities of national or "Schengen routing" of Internet data flows and what is referred to as a "Europe-only cloud" or "Schengen cloud." National or "Schengen routing" confines internet traffic within the national boundary or the Schengen Area so that data will not be sent via another country or region. An example of such a routing scheme is the proposed German-only "Internetz," which German telecommunication provider Deutsche Telekom announced in October 2013 it would build to keep German internet traffic within Germany's physical borders, followed by expansion to the Schengen Area (Kuner et al. 2015; Hon et al. 2016).

A "Europe-only cloud" practically means a system in which all cloud-processed data are physically located in Europe: that is, the data centers that hold servers or other equipment are geographically located in Europe. Such a cloud would be an integral part of "a kind of Schengen for data," which Thierry Bretton of EU cloud provider Atos (and France's former minister of economy, finance, and industry) proposed in August 2013 (Kuner et al. 2015; Hon et al. 2016). It should be noted that both the Schengen routing and Europe-only cloud are intended to constrain the physical location of data within Europe and, as such, could have significant impact on data exchanges between Europe and other parts of the world.

A main explicit objective of the Schengen routing and a Europe-only cloud is to limit access to European data by foreign intelligence authorities, thereby protecting European citizens' right to privacy. However, critics claim that these initiatives may be driven by economic motives, such as promotion of domestic providers of cloud and other internet-based services, development of domestic infrastructure, and the development of a single digital market in Europe (Hon et al. 2016).

Future of the Transatlantic Politics of Data Transfer

Recent developments in Europe suggest that transfer and use of personal data is likely to remain a source of friction between the EU and the US. The replacement of the Data Protection Directive with the General Data Protection Regulation would not put an end to extraterritorial application of EU data protection laws. Quite the contrary, with its enhanced scope of application and severe penalty for violation, the implementation of the General Data Protection Regulation is likely to cause controversy between the EU and other jurisdictions, most notably the US. A Europe-only cloud, if established, would constrain data location and transfers against the economic (and possibly security) interests of the US. Furthermore, the Schengen routing, if implemented, could lead to regionalization or Balkanization of the internet (Kuner et al. 2015), raising obstacles to the global flows of data the US has promoted. In sum, the transatlantic politics of data transfer would continue in the foreseeable future and might become even more complicated with the rise of new issues related to data protection and privacy.

Notes

1 The Commission has so far recognized Andorra, Argentina, Canada (commercial organizations), Faeroe Islands, Guernsey, Israel, Isle of Man, Jersey, New Zealand, Switzerland, and Uruguay as providing adequate protection. European Commission, "Commission decisions on the adequacy of the protection of personal data in third countries," http://ec.europa.eu/justice/data-protection/international-transfers/adequacy/index_en.htm, accessed September 26, 2016.

2 For a skeptical view of the EU's global influence in the field of data protection regulation, see (Young 2015).

3 The significance of territoriality suggests that "localization" of personal data could be a strategy to ensure compliance with "local" (e.g. European) data privacy

rules. For the EU, an "EU cloud" might provide a solution to the problem of the (mis)use of EU citizens' personal data in third countries. The US, however, is firmly against a requirement of local storage or processing of data and calls for a ban on it (Akhtar and Jones 2014).

4 In the Schengen Area, internal border controls have been abolished to allow for free movement of persons between the signatory countries of the Schengen Agreement, which was originally signed in 1985 and later incorporated into the EU *acquis*. Currently, the Schengen Area encompasses most EU member states, except for Bulgaria, Croatia, Cyprus, Ireland, Romania, and the United Kingdom. Some non-EU states, namely Iceland, Norway, Switzerland, and Liechtenstein, have also joined the Schengen Area. European Commission, "Schengen Area," http://ec.europa.eu/home-affairs/what-we-do/policies/borders-and-visas/schengen_en, accessed May 6, 2017.

5 The idea of a virtual Schengen area was first floated in February 2011, during a discussion of cybercrime at a Joint Meeting of the EU's Law Enforcement and Customs Cooperation Working Parties (Kuner et al. 2015).

References

Agnew, J. (1994) "The territorial trap: the geographical assumptions of international relations theory," *Review of International Political Economy* 1, 1, pp. 53–80.

Ahearn, R. J. (2007) "Trade conflict and US–European Union economic relationship," Congressional Research Service (CRS) Report for Congress, April 11.

Akhtar, S. I. and Jones, V. C. (2014) "Transatlantic Trade and Investment Partnership (TTIP) negotiations," Congressional Research Service Report for Congress, February 4. Available at https://fas.org/sgp/crs/row/R43387.pdf.

Archick, K. (2010) "US–EU cooperation against terrorism," Congressional Research Service (CRS) Report for Congress, July 9. Available at www.fas.org/sgp/crs/row/RS22030.pdf.

Archick, K. (2016) "US–EU cooperation against terrorism," Congressional Research Service (CRS) Report, March 2. Available at www.statewatch.org/news/2016/mar/usa-crs-eu-usa-c-t-cooperation.pdf.

Argomaniz, J. (2009) "When the EU is the 'norm-taker': The Passenger Name Records Agreement and the EU's internalization of US border security norms," *European Integration*, 31, 11, pp. 119–136.

Article 29 Working Party (1999) "Opinion 2/99 on the adequacy of the 'International Safe Harbor Principles' issued by the US Department of Commerce on 19th April 1999," 5047/99/EN/final WP 19, adopted on May 3.

Article 29 Data Protection Working Party (2000) "Opinion 4/2000 on the level of protection provided by the 'Safe Harbor Principles'," adopted on May 16.

Article 29 Data Protection Working Party (2002) "Opinion 6/2002 on transmission of Passenger Manifest Information and other data from airlines to the United States," adopted on October 24.

Article 29 Data Protection Working Party (2003) "Opinion 4/2003 on the level of protection ensured in the US for the transfer of passengers' data," adopted on June 13.

Article 29 Data Protection Working Party (2004a) "Opinion 2/2004 on the adequate protection of personal data contained in the PNR of air passengers to be transferred to the United States' Bureau of Customs and Border Protection (US CBP)," adopted on January 29.

Article 29 Data Protection Working Party (2004b) "Opinion 6/2004 on the implementation of the Commission decision of 14-V-2004 on the adequate protection of personal data contained in the passenger name records of air passengers transferred to the United States' Bureau of Customs and Border

Protection, and of the Agreement between the European Community and the United States of America on the processing and transfer of PNR data by air carriers to the United States Department of Homeland Security, Bureau of Customs and Border Protection," adopted on June 22.

Article 29 Data Protection Working Party (2006) "Opinion 10/2006 on the processing of personal data by the Society for Worldwide Interbank Financial Telecommunication (SWIFT)," adopted on November 22.

Article 29 Data Protection Working Party (2014a) "Opinion 04/2014 on surveillance of electronic communications for intelligence and national security purposes," adopted on April 10.

Article 29 Data Protection Working Party (2014b) "Joint Statement of the European data protection authorities assembled in the Article 29 Working Party," adopted on November 26.

Article 29 Data Protection Working Party (2016) "Opinion 01/2016 on the EU: US Privacy Shield draft adequacy decision," adopted on April 13.

Article 29 Data Protection Working Party and Working Party on Police and Justice (2007) "Joint opinion on the proposal for a Council Framework Decision on the use of Passenger Name Record (PNR) for law enforcement purposes, presented by the Commission on 6 November 2007," adopted on December 5 by the Article 29 Working Party and on December 18 by the Working Party on Police and Justice.

Article 29 Working Party (2015) "Statement of the Article 29 Working Party," Brussels, October 16.

Asahi Shimbun (2008) "PCI zen-shacho-ra taiho [former PCI president and others arrested]" August 5.

Bach, D. and Newman, A. L. (2007) "The European regulatory state and global public policy: micro-institutions, macro-influence," *Journal of European Public Policy* 14, 6, pp. 827–846.

Bach, D. and Newman, A. (2010) "Governing Lipitor and lipstick: Capacity, sequencing, and power in international pharmaceutical and cosmetics regulation," *Review of International Political Economy* 17, 4, pp. 665–695.

Baker, P. (2017) "Trump abandons Trans-Pacific Partnership, Obama's signature trade deal," *New York Times*, January 23.

Bąkowski, P. and Voronova, S. (2015) "The proposed EU passenger name records (PNR) directive: Revived in the new security context," briefing, European Parliamentary Research Service (EPRS), April. Available at www.europarl.europa.eu/EPRS/EPRS-Briefing-554215-The-EU-PNR-Proposal-FINAL.pdf.

Balzacq, T. (2008) "The policy tools of securitization: Information exchange, EU foreign and interior policies," *Journal of Common Market Studies*, 46, 1, pp. 75–100.

BBC News (2012) "Countries rally against EU carbon tax on airlines, February 21. Available at www.bbc.com/news/world-europe-17114312.

Bennett, C. J. (1992) *Regulating Privacy: Data Protection and Public Policy in Europe and the United States*, Ithaca, NY; London: Cornell University Press.

Bennett, C. J. (1998) "Convergence revisited: Toward a global policy for the protection of personal data?", in P. E. Agre and M. Rotenberg, eds, *Technology and Privacy: The New Landscape*, Cambridge, MA; London: MIT Press, pp. 99–123.

Bennett, C. J. (2005) 'What happens when you book an airline ticket? The collection and processing of passenger data post-9/11', in E. Zureik and M. B. Salter, eds, *Global Surveillance and Policing: Borders, Security, Identity*, Cullompton, Devon: Willan Publishing, pp. 115–121.

Bennett, C. J. and Raab, C. D. (2006) *The Governance of Privacy: Policy Instruments in Global Perspective*, Cambridge, MA; London: MIT Press.

Bessette, R. and Haufler, V. (2001) "Against all odds: Why there is no international information regime," *International Studies Perspectives*, 2, 1, pp. 69–92.

Biersteker, T. (2002) "State, sovereignty and territory," in W. Carlsnaes, T. Risse, and B. A. Simmons, eds, *Handbook of International Relations*, London: Sage, pp. 157–176.

Blenkinsop, P. (2016) "US trade talks in deep freeze after Trump win, says EU," *Reuters*, November 11.

Borger, J. (2016) "Transatlantic trade deal 'not realistic' under Trump, German official says," *Guardian*, November 15.

Bolkestein, F. (2003) "EU/US talks on transfers of airline passengers' personal data," Address to European Parliament Committee on Citizens' Freedoms and Rights, Justice and Home Affairs, Brussels.

Bolkestein, F. (2003) "EU/US talks on transfers of airline passengers' personal data," Address to European Parliament Committees on Citizens' Freedoms and Rights, Justice and Home Affairs and Legal Affairs and the International Market, Strasbourg.

Broberg, M. P. "The European Commission's extraterritorial powers in merger control," *International and Comparative Law Quarterly*, 49, 1, pp. 172–182.

Büthe, T. and Mattli, W. (2011) *The New Global Rulers: The Privatization of Regulation in World Economy*, Princeton: Princeton University Press.

Cairncross, F. (1997) *The Death of Distance: How the Communications Revolution will Change Our Lives*, London: Orion Business.

Caldwell, S. L. (2008) "Supply chain security: Challenges to scanning 100 percent of US-bound cargo containers." Available at www.gao.gov/new.items/d08533t.pdf.

Chander, A. and Lê, U. P. (2015) "Data nationalism," *Emory Law Journal*, 64, pp. 677–739.

Charlesworth, A. (2000) "Clash of data Titans? US and EU data privacy regulation," *European Public Law*, 6, 2, pp. 253–274.

Cîrlig, Carmen-Cristina (2016) "EU–US cooperation in Justice and Home Affairs: An overview," briefing, European Parliamentary Research Service (EPRS), April. Available at www.europarl.europa.eu/RegData/etudes/BRIE/2016/580892/EPRS_BRI(2016)580892_EN.pdf.

Clinton, W. J. and A. Gore, Jr. (1997) "A framework for global electronic commerce," July 1. Available at http://clinton4.nara.gov/WH/New/Commerce/read.html.

Coglianese, C. (2000) "Globalization and the design of international institutions," in J. S. Nye and J. D. Donahue, eds, *Governance in a Globalizing World*, Washington, DC: Brookings Institution Press, pp. 297–318.

Council of the European Union (2004) "EU–US Declaration on Combating Terrorism," adopted at the EU–US summit, Dromoland Castle, June 24.

Council of the European Union (2005) "Council declaration on the EU response to the London bombings," Extraordinary Council Meeting, Justice and Home Affairs, Brussels, July 13.

Council of the European Union (2010a) "EU–US agreement on the transfer of financial messaging data for purposes of the Terrorist Finance Tracking Programme," press release. Available at www.consilium.europa.eu/uedocs/cms_data/docs/pressdata/en/jha/112850.pdf.

Council of the European Union (2010b) "Council Decision of 13 July 2010 on the conclusion of the Agreement between the European Union and the United States of America on the processing and transfer of Financial Messaging Data from the European Union to the United States for the purposes of the Terrorist Finance Tracking Program." Available at eur-lex.europa.eu/legal-content/EN/TXT/?uri=OJ%3AJOL_2010_195_R_0003_01.

Council of the European Union (2012) "3162nd Council meeting, Justice and Home Affairs," press release, Luxembourg, April 26/27.

Council of the European Union (2013) "Directives for the negotiation on the Transatlantic Trade and Investment Partnership between the European Union and the United States of America," Brussels, June 17.

Council of the European Union (2015a) "Outcome of the Council Meeting, 3420th Council meeting: Foreign affairs, trade issues," Brussels, November 27.

Council of the European Union (2015b), "Information by the Commission on the PNR legislation adopted by Mexico and the Republic of Argentina requesting the transfer of PNR data from the EU," Brussels, March 5.

Council of the European Union (2016a) "EU–South Korea free trade agreement concluded," press release, October 1. Available at www.consilium.europa.eu/en/press/press-releases/2015/10/01-korea-free-trade/.

Council of the European Union (2016b) "Umbrella agreement: EU ready to conclude deal with the US," press release, December 2. Available at www.consilium.europa.eu/en/press/press-releases/2016/12/02-umbrella-agreement/.

Council of the European Union (2016c) "Council adopts EU Passenger Name Record (PNR) directive," press release, April 21. Available at www.consilium.europa.eu/en/press/press-releases/2016/04/21-council-adopts-eu-pnr-directive/.

Court of Justice of the European Union (CJEU) (2015) "The Court of Justice declares that the Commission's US Safe Harbour Decision is invalid," press release, October 6. Available at https://curia.europa.eu/jcms/upload/docs/application/pdf/2015-10/cp150117en.pdf.

Dalton, M. (2016) "France seeks to end US–EU trade talks," *Wall Street Journal*, August 30.

Darrough, M. N. (2010) "The FCPA and the OECD Convention: Some lessons from the US experience," *Journal of Business Ethics*, 93, 2, pp. 255–276.

de Goede, M. (2012a) "The SWIFT affair and the global politics of European security," *Journal of Common Market Studies*, 50, 2, pp. 214–230 (published online November 8, 2011).

de Goede, M. (2012b) *Speculative Security: The Politics of Pursuing Terrorist Monies*, Minneapolis; London: University of Minnesota Press.

De Hert, P. and Bellanova, R. (2008) "Data protection from a transatlantic perspective: The EU and US move towards an international data protection agreement?" Study for the European Parliament, PE 408.320.

Deibert, J. R. (2002) "Circuits of power: Security in the internet environment," in J. N. Rosenau and J. P. Singh, eds, *Information Technologies and Global Politics: The Changing Scope of Power and Governance*, New York: State University of New York Press, pp. 115–142.

Deibert, J. R., Palfrey, J., Rohozinski, R., and Zittrain, J. (2011) *Access Contested: Security, Identity, and Resistance in Asian Cyberspace*, Cambridge, MA: MIT Press.

Den Boer, M. and Monar, J. (2002) "Keynote article: 11 September and the challenge of global terrorism to the EU as a security actor," *Journal of Common Market Studies*, 40, Annual Review, pp. 11–28.

Devuyst, Y. (2000) "Toward a multilateral competition policy regime?" *Global Governance*, 6, 3, pp. 319–338.

Drezner, D. W. (2007) *All Politics is Global: Explaining International Regulatory Regime*, Princeton: Princeton University Press.

European Commission (2000a), "Data protection: Commission endorses 'safe harbor' arrangement with US," press release IP/00/301, March 29.

European Commission (2000b) "Commission Decision of 26 July 2000 pursuant to Directive 95/46/EC of the European Parliament and of the Council on the adequacy of the protection provided by the Safe Harbour privacy principles and related frequently asked questions issued by the US Department of Commerce," 2000/520/EC.

European Commission (2003a) "Customs: Commission proposes to negotiate EU/US co-operation arrangements for transport security," press release IP/03/108, January 23.

European Commission (2003b) "Customs: Commission welcomes Council authorisation to negotiate with US on transport security cooperation," press release IP/03/399, March 18.

European Commission (2003c) "Airline passenger data transfers from the EU to the United States (Passenger Name Record) frequently asked questions," press release, March 12. Available at http://europa.eu/rapid/pressReleasesAction.do?reference=MEMO/03/53&format=HTML&aged=1&language=EN&guiLanguage=en.

European Commission (2003d) "Communication from the Commission to the Council and the Parliament, transfer of Air Passenger Name Record (PNR) data: A global EU approach," COM(2003) 826, December 16.

European Commission (2004a) "Customs: Commission welcomes signature of agreement with United States on expanding cooperation to trade security," press release IP/04/525, April 22.

European Commission (2004b) "Customs: EU and US adopt measures to strengthen maritime container security," press release IP/04/1360, November 15.

European Commission (2004c) "Commission secures guarantees for protecting personal data of transatlantic air passengers," press release IP/04/650, May 17.

European Commission (2007a) "USA to take account of EU data protection principles to process data received from Swift," press release IP/07/968, June 28.

European Commission (2007b) "The SWIFT case and the American Terrorist Finance Tracking Program," press release MEMO/07/266, June 28.

European Commission (2007c) "Proposal for a Council Framework Decision on the use of Passenger Name Record (PNR) for law enforcement purposes," COM (2007) 654 final, Brussels, November 6.

European Commission (2009a) "Integration of biometric features in passports and travel documents," Brussels, September 2. Available at http://europa.eu/legislation_summaries/justice_freedom_security/fight_against_terrorism/l14154_en.htm.

European Commission (2009b) "EU Review of the United States' 'Terrorist Finance Tracking Programme' confirms privacy safeguards," press release IP/09/264, February 17. Available at http://europa.eu/rapid/pressReleasesAction.do?reference=IP/09/264&format=HTML&aged=0&language=EN&guiLanguage=en.

European Commission (2010) "Communication from the Commission on the global approach to transfers of Passenger Name Record (PNR) data to third countries," COM/2010/ 0492 final, September 21.

European Commission (2011a) "New EU–US agreement on PNR improves data protection and fights crime and terrorism," press release, November 17. Available at http://europa.eu/rapid/pressReleasesAction.do?reference=IP/11/1368.

European Commission (2011b) "Communication from the Commission to the European Parliament and the Council A European terrorist finance tracking system: available options," COM(2011) 429 final, July 13.

European Commission (2011c) "Frequently Asked Questions: The new EU–US agreement on the transfer of Passenger Name Record (PNR) data," press release MEMO/11/797, November 17.

European Commission (2011d) "European Commission (2011d) "Proposal for a directive of the European Parliament and of the Council on the use of Passenger Name Record data for the prevention, detection, investigation and prosecution of terrorist offences and serious crime," COM(2011) 0032 final, February 2.

European Commission (2012a) "Communication from the Commission to the European Parliament, the Council, the European Economic and Social Committee and the Committee of the Regions Safeguarding Privacy in a Connected World A European Data Protection Framework for the 21st Century," COM (2012) 09 final, January 25.

European Commission (2012b) "Commission proposes a comprehensive reform of data protection rules to increase users' control of their data and to cut costs for businesses," press release, Brussels, January 25.

European Commission (2013a) "Communication from the Commission to the European Parliament and the Council: A European terrorist finance tracking system (EU TFTS)," COM(2013) 842 final, Brussels, November 27.

European Commission (2013b) "Communication from the Commission to the European Parliament and the Council rebuilding trust in EU–US data flows," COM(2013) 846 final, Brussels, November 27.

European Commission (2013c) "Communication from the Commission to the European Parliament and the Council on the functioning of the Safe Harbour from the perspective of EU citizens and companies established in the EU," COM (2013) 847 final, November 27.

European Commission (2013d) "EU–US agreements: Commission reports on TFTP and PNR," press release, Brussels, November 27. Available at http://europa.eu/rapid/press-release_IP-13-1160_en.htm (accessed July 31, 2015).

European Commission (2013e), "Restoring trust in EUUS data flows: Frequently Asked Questions," MEMO/13/1059, November 27.

European Commission (2014) "Reducing emissions from aviation." Last update: December 12. Available at http://ec.europa.eu/clima/policies/transport/aviation/index_en.htm.

European Commission (2015a) "Q&A: Guidance on transatlantic data transfers following the Schrems ruling," MEMO/15/6014, November 6.

European Commission (2015b) "Joint Statement: Beginning of negotiations between Mexico and the European Union on PNR data transmission," Mexico City, July 14.

European Commission (2016a) "EU Commission and United States agree on new framework for transatlantic data flows: EU–US Privacy Shield," press release IP/16/216, Strasbourg, February 2.

European Commission (2016b) "European Commission unveils EU–US Privacy Shield," press release, February 29.

European Commission (2016c) "Communication from the Commission to the European Parliament and the Council Transatlantic Data Flows: Restoring Trust through Strong Safeguards," COM(2016) 117 final, Brussels, February 29.

European Commission (2016d) "European Commission launches EU–US Privacy Shield: Stronger protection for transatlantic data flows," press release IP/16/2461, Brussels, 12 July.

European Commission (2016e) "Commission implementing decision of 12.7.2016 pursuant to Directive 95/46/EC of the European Parliament and of the Council on the adequacy of the protection provided by the EU–US Privacy Shield," C (2016) 4176 final, Brussels, 12 July.

European Commission (2016f) "Trade in Services Agreement (TiSA)," fact sheet, September 26.

European Commission (2016g) "Questions and Answers on the EU–US data protection "Umbrella Agreement," fact sheet, December 1.

European Commission (2016h) "The Transatlantic Trade and Investment Partnership (TTIP): State of play." Available at http://trade.ec.europa.eu/doclib/docs/2016/april/tradoc_154477.pdf.

European Commission (2017) "US–EU joint report on TTIP progress to date," January 17.

European Council (2004) "Declaration on combating terrorism," Brussels, March 25.

European Council (2005) "The Hague Programme: Strengthening freedom, security and justice in the European Union," 2005/C 053/1, March 3.

European Council (2010) "The Stockholm Programme: An open and secure Europe serving and protecting citizens," 2010/C 115/01, May 4.

European Council (2015) "Informal meeting of the Heads of State or Government, Brussels, 12 February 2015: Statement by the members of the European Council, press release and statement." Available at www.consilium.europa.eu/en/press/press-releases/2015/02/150212-european-council-statement-fight-against-terrorism/.

European Council (2016a) "Council adopts EU Passenger Name Record (PNR) directive," press release, 21 April.

European Council (2016b) "Enhanced data protection rights for EU citizens in law enforcement cooperation: EU and US sign 'Umbrella agreement'," press release, June 2.

European Data Protection Supervisor (EDPS) (2007a) "EDPS calls on ECB to ensure that European payment systems comply with data protection law," press release EDPS/07/1, February 1.

European Data Protection Supervisor (EDPS) (2007b) "Opinion of the European Data Protection Supervisor on the draft Proposal for a Council Framework Decision on the use of Passenger Name Record (PNR) for law enforcement purposes," 2008/C 110/01, December 20.

European Data Protection Supervisor (EDPS) (2014) "Opinion of the European Data Protection Supervisor on the Communication from the Commission to the European Parliament and the Council on 'Rebuilding Trust in EU–US Data Flows' and on the Communication from the Commission to the European Parliament and the Council on 'the Functioning of the Safe Harbour from the Perspective of EU Citizens and Companies Established in the EU'," February 20. Available at https://edps.europa.eu/sites/edp/files/publication/14-02-20_eu_us_rebuliding_trust_en.pdf.

European Data Protection Supervisor (EDPS) (2015) "Second Opinion on the Proposal for a Directive of the European Parliament and of the Council on the use of Passenger Name Record data for the prevention, detection, investigation and prosecution of terrorist offences and serious crime," Opinion 5/2015, September 24.

European Digital Rights (EDRi) (2016) "Trade in Services Agreement: EDRi's position," January. Available at https://edri.org/files/TiSA_Position_Jan2016e.pdf.

European Parliament (2000) "European Parliament resolution on the Draft Commission Decision on the adequacy of the protection provided by the Safe Harbour Privacy Principles and related Frequently Asked Questions issued by the US Department of Commerce," A5–0177/2000, Strasbourg, July.

European Parliament (2006) "Resolution on the interception of bank transfer data from the SWIFT system by the US secret services," P6_TA-PROV(2006)0317, July 6.

European Parliament (2008) "European Parliament resolution of 20 November 2008 on the proposal for a Council framework decision on the use of Passenger Name Record (PNR) for law enforcement purposes," P6_TA(2008)0561, November 20.

European Parliament (2009a) "European Parliament resolution of 26 March 2009 on the state of transatlantic relations in the aftermath of the US elections," P6_TA (2009)0193, March 26.

European Parliament (2009b) "Resolution of 17 September 2009 on the envisaged international agreement to make available to the United States Treasury Department financial payment messaging data to prevent and combat terrorism and terrorist financing," P7_TA(2009)0016, September 17.

European Parliament (2010) "Parliament gives green light for SWIFT II," press release. Available at www.europarl.europa.eu/pdfs/news/expert/infopress/20100707IPR78054/20100707IPR78054_en.pdf.

European Parliament (2011), "US Attorney General in EP to talk about data protection," News, September 21, Available at www.europarl.europa.eu/news/en/headlines/world/20110916STO26855/us-attorney-general-in-ep-to-talk-about-data-protection.

European Parliament (2012a) "Transfer of air passengers' data to the US: What's at stake?" background note. Available at www.europarl.europa.eu/pdfs/news/expert/background/20120326BKG41893/20120326BKG41893_en.pdf.

European Parliament (2012b) "MEPs battle it out over controversial agreement to transfer air passenger data to the US," April 16. Available at www.europarl.europa.eu/news/en/news-room/20120413STO42885/meps-battle-it-out-over-controversial-air-passenger-data-agreement.

European Parliament (2012c) "Parliament gives green light to air passenger data deal with the US," press release. Available at www.europarl.europa.eu/news/en/news-room/20120419IPR43404/parliament-gives-green-light-to-air-passenger-data-deal-with-the-us.

European Parliament (2013a) "Resolution of 4 July 2013 on the US National Security Agency surveillance programme, surveillance bodies in various member states and their impact on EU citizens' privacy," P7_TA(2013)0322.

European Parliament (2013b) "Resolution of 23 October 2013 on the suspension of the TFTP agreement as a result of US National Security Agency surveillance," P7_TA(2013)0449.

European Parliament (2014) "Resolution of 12 March 2014 on the US NSA surveillance programme, surveillance bodies in various member states and their impact on EU citizens' fundamental rights and on transatlantic cooperation in Justice and Home Affairs," P7_TA-PROV(2014)0230.

European Parliament (2015a) "European Parliament resolution of 8 July 2015 containing the European Parliament's recommendations to the European Commission on the negotiations for the Transatlantic Trade and Investment Partnership (TTIP)," P8_TA(2015)0252.

European Parliament (2015b) "European Parliament resolution of 11 February 2015 on anti-terrorism measures," P8_TA(2015)0032.

European Parliament (2015c) "European Parliament resolution of 9 July 2015 on the European Agenda on Security," P8_TA(2015)0269.

European Parliament (2015d) "European Parliament resolution of 25 November 2015 on the prevention of radicalisation and recruitment of European citizens by terrorist organisations," P8_TA(2015)0410.

European Parliament (2016a) "Parliament backs EU directive on use of Passenger Name Records (PNR)," press release 14-04-2016.

European Parliament (2016b) "Resolution of 26 May 2016 on transatlantic data flows," P8_TA-PROV(2016)0233.

European Parliament (2016c) "The Maastricht and Amsterdam treaties," fact sheet. Available at www.europarl.europa.eu/ftu/pdf/en/FTU_1.1.3.pdf.

European Parliament (2016d) "EU Passenger Name Record (PNR) directive: An overview," background note, 01-06-2016.

European Parliament (2016e) "European Parliament resolution of 3 February 2016 containing the European Parliament's recommendations to the Commission on the negotiations for the Trade in Services Agreement (TiSA)," P8_TA(2016)0041.

Farrell, H. (2003) "Constructing the international foundations of e-commerce: The EU–US Safe Harbor arrangement," *International Organization*, 57, 2, pp. 277–306.

Farrell, H. (2005) "The political economy of the internet and e-commerce," in R. Stubbs and G. R. D. Underhill, eds, *Political Economy and the Changing Global Order*, 3rd ed., Oxford: Oxford University Press, pp. 211–221.

Farrell, H. and Newman, A. (2015) "The new politics of interdependence: Cross-national layering in Trans-Atlantic regulatory disputes," *Comparative Political Studies*, 48, 4, pp. 497–526.

Farrell, S. (2016) "France demands an end to TTIP talks," *The Guardian*, August 30.

Fefer, R. F. (2016) "US trade in services: Trends and policy issues," Congressional Research Service Report, R43291, December 6.

Fefer, R. F. (2017) "Trade in Services Agreement (TiSA) Negotiations: Overview and Issues for Congress," Congressional Research Service Report, R44354, January 3.

Fergusson, I. F. and Williams, B. R. (2016) "The Trans-Pacific Partnership (TPP): Key provisions and issues for Congress," Congressional Research Service Report, R44489, June 14.

Fleming, J. (2013) "Reding warns data protection could derail US trade talks," *EurActive*, http://beta.euractiv.com/section/digital/news/reding-warns-data-protection-could-derail-us-trade-talks/.

Fontanella-Khan, J. (2013) "Data protection ruled out of EU–US trade talks," *Financial Times*, November 4.

Fuster, G., de Hert, P., and Gutwirth, S. (2008) "SWIFT and the vulnerability of transatlantic data transfers," *International Review of Law, Computers & Technology*, 22(1–2) pp. 191–202.

Gellman, B. and Poltras, L. (2013) "US, British intelligence mining data from nine US internet companies in broad secret program," *Washington Post*, June 7.

Gellman, R. (1999) "Conflict and overlap in privacy regulation: National, international, and private," in B. Kahin and C. Nesson, eds, *Borders in Cyberspace: Information Policy and the Global Information Infrastructure*, Cambridge, MA; London: MIT Press, pp. 255–282.

Gellman, R. and Dixon, P. (2011) *Online Privacy: A Reference Handbook*, Santa Barbara: ABC-CLIO.

General Secretariat of the Council of the EU (2009) "Information Note, EU–US agreement on the processing and transfer of financial messaging data for purposes of the US Terrorist Finance Tracking Programme (TFTP): Questions and answers," information note. Available at www.consilium.europa.eu/uedocs/cms_data/docs/pressdata/en/jha/111559.pdf.

Greenleaf, G. (2013) "Data Protection in a globalized network," in I. Brown, ed., *Research Handbook on Governance of the Internet*, Cheltenham: Edward Elgar, pp. 221–259.

Greenleaf, G. (2016) "The TPP and other free trade agreements: Faustian bargain for privacy?" UNSW Law Research Paper no. 2016-08, University of New South Wales, Sidney.

Greenwald, G. and Ewen MacAskill (2013) "NSA Prism program taps in to user data of Apple, Google and others," *The Guardian*, June 7.

Hailbronner, K., Papakonstantinou, V. and Kau, M. (2008) "The Agreement on Passenger Data Transfer (PNR) and the EU–US cooperation in data communication," *International Migration*, 46, 2, pp. 187–197.

Heisenberg, D. (2005) *Negotiating Privacy: the European Union, the United States, and Personal Data Protection*, Boulder, CO; London: Lynne Reinner.

Hon, W. K., Millard, C., Singh, J., Walden, I., and Crowcroft, J. (2016) "Policy, legal and regulatory implications of a Europe-only cloud," *International Journal of Law and Information Technology*, 24, pp. 251–278.

Hosein, I. (2004) "The source of laws: Policy dynamics in a digital and terrorized world," *The Information Society* 20, 3, pp. 187–199.

House of Lords European Union Committee (2007) *The EU/US Passenger Name Record (PNR) Agreement Report with Evidence*, London: The Stationary Office. Available at www.publications.parliament.uk/pa/ld200607/ldselect/ldeucom/108/108.pdf.

Hufbauer, G. C. and Cimino-Isaacs, C. (2015) "How will TP and TTIP change the WTO systems?" *Journal of International Economic Law*, 18, pp. 679–696.

Hufbauer, G. C., Schott, J. J., Elliott, K. A. and Oegg, B. (2007) *Economic Sanctions Reconsidered*, 3rd ed., Washington, DC: Peterson Institute for International Economics.

Hurley, D. and Mayer-Schönberger, V. (2000) "Information Policy and Governance," in J. S. Nye and J. D. Donahue, eds, *Governance in a Globalizing World*, Washington, DC: Brooking Institution Press, pp. 330–346.

International Telecommunication Union (ITU) (2015) "ITU releases 2015 ICT figures Statistics confirm ICT revolution of the past 15 years," press release. Available at www.itu.int/net/pressoffice/press_releases/2015/17.aspx#.WP1qDE2weUk.

Kaczmarek, S. C. and Newman, A. L. (2011) "The long arm of the law: Extraterritoriality and the national implementation of foreign bribery legislation," *International Organization*, 65, pp. 745–770.

Kahler, M. (2006) 'Territoriality and conflict in an era of globalization', in M. Kahler and B. F. Walter, eds, *Territoriality and Conflict in an Era of Globalization*, Cambridge: Cambridge University Press, pp. 1–21.

Kahler, M. and Lake, D. A. (2009) "Economic integration and global governance: Why so little supranationalism?" in W. Mattli and N. Woods, eds, *The Politics of Global Regulation*, Princeton: Princeton University Press, pp. 242–275.

Kirby, M. (2011) "The history, achievement and future of the 1980 OECD guidelines on privacy," *International Data Privacy Law*, 1, 1, pp. 6–14.

Klosek, J. (2007) *The War on Privacy*, Westport, CT; London: Praeger.

Kobrin, S. J. (2004) "Safe harbours are hard to find: the trans-Atlantic data privacy disputes, territorial jurisdiction and global governance," *Review of International Studies*, 30, 1, pp. 111–131.

Kuner, C. (2013) *Transborder Data Flows and Data Privacy Law*, Oxford: Oxford University Press.

Kuner, C. (2015) "Extraterritoriality and regulation of international data transfers in EU data protection law," *International Data Privacy Law*, 5, 4, pp. 235–245.

Kuner, C. (2016) "Reality and illusion in EU data transfer regulation post-Schrems," University of Cambridge Faculty of Law Research Paper no. 14.

Kuner, C., Cate, F. H., Millard, C., and Svantesson, D. J. B. (2013) "The exteraterritoriality of data privacy laws: An explosive issue yet to detonate," *International Data Privacy Law*, 3, 3, pp. 147–148.

Kuner, C., Cate, F. H., Millard, C., Svantesson, D. J. B., and Lynskey, O. (2015) "Internet Balkanization gathers pace: Is privacy the real driver?" *International data Privacy Law*, 5, 1, pp. 1–2.

Lattman, P. (2012) "Tiger Asia founder, onetime star, admits to his fund's improper trading," *New York Times*, late edition (East Coast) [New York], December 13.

Lichtblau, E. and Risen, J. (2006) "Bank data sifted in secret by US to block terror," *New York Times*, June 23, A.1.

Loeffler, R. L. (2009) "Bank shots: How the financial system can isolate rogues", *Foreign Affairs*, 88, 2, pp. 101–110.

Long, W. J. and Quek, M. P. (2002) "Personal data privacy protection in an age of globalization: The US–EU Safe Harbor compromise," *Journal of European Public Policy*, 9, 3, pp. 325–344.

Malmström, C. (2010) "Statement on the draft agreement with the United States on the Terrorist Finance Tracking Programme (TFTP)," press statement at the occasion of the presentation of the state of play of the negotiations of the draft agreement on the TFTP agreement to the LIBE Committee of the European Parliament LIBE.

Manners, I. (2002) "Normative power Europe: A contradiction in terms?" *Journal of Common Market Studies*, 40, 2, pp. 235–258.

McKinsey Global Institute (2016) "Digital globalization: The new era of global flows." Available at www.mckinsey.com/business-functions/digital-mckinsey/our-insights/digital-globalization-the-new-era-of-global-flows.

Miller, S. E. (2010) "The War on Terror and international order: Strategic choice and global governance," in A. S. Alexanderoff and A. F. Cooper, eds, *Rising States, Rising Institutions: Challenges for Global Governance*, Washington, DC: Brookings Institution Press, pp. 266–293.

Monar, J. (2010) "The rejection of the EU–US SWIFT Interim Agreement by the European Parliament: A historic vote and its implication," *European Foreign Affairs Review*, 15, pp. 143–151.

Monteleone, S. (2016) "Completing the adoption of an EU PNR Directive," European Parliamentary Research Service, April 7. Available at www.europarl.europa.eu/thinktank/en/document.html?reference=EPRS_ATA(2016)580886.

Newman, A.L. (2008a), "Building transnational civil liberties: Transgovernmental entrepreneurs and the European Data Privacy Directive," *International Organization*, 62, 1, pp. 103–130.

Newman, A. L. (2008b) *Protectors of Privacy: Regulating Personal Data in the Global Economy*, Ithaca; London: Cornell University Press.

Newman, A. L. (2010) "International organization control under conditions of dual delegation: a transgovernmental politics approach," in D. D. Avant, M. Finnemore, and S. Sell, eds, *Who Governs the Globe?*Cambridge: Cambridge University Press, pp. 131–152.

Newman, A. L. (2011) "Transatlantic fight fights: Multi-level governance, actor entrepreneurship and international anti-terrorism cooperation," *Review of International Political Economy*, 18, 4, pp. 481–505.

Online Privacy Alliance (OPA) (1998) "OPA white paper: Online consumer data privacy in the United States," November 19. Available at www.privacyalliance.org/news/12031998-5.shtml.

Organisation for Economic Cooperation and Development (OECD) (2013) *The OECD Privacy Framework*, Paris: OECD Publishing.

Pawlak, P. (2009a) "The external dimension of the area of Freedom, Security and Justice: Hijacker or hostage of cross-pillarization?" *Journal of European Integration*, 31, 1, pp. 25–44.

Pawlak, P. (2009b) "Made in the USA? The influence of the US on the EU'sdData protection regime," Centre for European Policy Studies. Available at www.ceps.eu/ceps/download/2680.

Posner, E. (2009) "Making rules for global finance: Transatlantic regulatory cooperation at the turn of the Millennium", *International Organization*, 63, 4, pp. 665–699.

Privacy International (2004) "Transferring privacy: The transfer of passenger records and the abdication of privacy protection." Available at www.privacyinternational.org/issues/terrorism/rpt/transferringprivacy.pdf.

Puccio, L. (2016) "EU–US negotiations on TTIP: A survey of current issues," European Parliamentary Research Service (EPRS). Available at www.europarl.europa.eu/RegData/etudes/IDAN/2016/586606/EPRS_IDA%282016%29586606_EN.pdf.

Putnam, T. L. (2009) "Courts without borders: Domestic sources of US extraterritoriality in the regulatory sphere," *International Organization*, 63, pp. 459–490.

Quesada Gámez, M. and Mincheva, E. (2012) "No data without protection? Rethinking transatlantic information exchange for law enforcement purposes after Lisbon," in Cardwell, P. J., ed., *EU External Relations La wand Policy in the Post-Lisbon Era*, The Hague: T.M.C. Asser Press, pp. 287–312.

Raustiala, K. (2009) *Does Constitution Follow the Flag? The Evolution of Extraterritoriality in American Law*, Oxford: Oxford University Press.

Rees, W. (2006) *Transatlantic Counter-terrorism: The New Imperative*, London; New York: Routledge.

Reidenberg, J. R. (1999) "Governing networks and rule-making in cyberspace," in B. Kahin and C. Nesson, eds, *Borders in Cyberspace: Information Policy and the Global Information Infrastructure*, Cambridge, MA; London: MIT Press, pp. 84–105.

Reidenberg, J. R.(2000) "Resolving conflicting international data privacy rules in cyberspace," *Stanford Law Review*, 52, pp. 1315–1371.

Reitinger, P. R. (2000) "Encryption, anonymity and markets: Law enforcement and technology in a free market virtual world," in D. Thomas and B. D. Loader, eds, *Cybercrime: Law Enforcement, Security and Surveillance in the Information Age*, London; New York: Routledge, pp. 132–152.

Roberts, H. and JohnPalfrey, J. (2010) "The EU Data Retention Directive in an era of internet surveillance," in R. Deibert, J. Palfrey, R. Rohozinski, and J. Zittrain, eds, *Access Controlled: The Shaping of Power, Rights, and Rule in Cyberspace*, Cambridge, MA; London: MIT Press, pp. 35–53.

Romero, J. (2003) "Prevention of maritime terrorism: The Container Security Initiative," *Chicago Journal of International Law*, 4, 2, pp. 597–605.

Rotenberg, M. (2003) "Privacy and Secrecy After September 11," in R. Latham, ed., *Bombs and Bandwidth: The Emerging Relationship between Information Technology and Security*, New York: The New Press, pp. 132–142.

Ryngaert, C. (2015) "Symposium issue on extraterritoriality and EU data protection," *International Data Privacy Law*, 5, 4, pp. 221–225.

Santolli, J. (2008) "The Terrorist Finance Tracking Program: Illuminating the shortcomings of the European Union's antiquated Data Privacy Directive," *George Washington International Law Review*, 40, pp. 553–582.

Sassen, S. (2006) *Territory, Authority, Rights: From Medieval to Global Assemblages*, Princeton; Oxford: Princeton University Press.

Scott, C. (2005) "Between the old and new: Innovation in the regulation of internet gambling", in J. Black, M. Lodge, and M. Thatcher, eds, *Regulatory Innovation: A Comparative Analysis*, Cheltenham, UK; Northampton, MA: Edward Elgar, pp. 114–137.

Scott, J. (2014a) "The new EU 'extraterritoriality'," *Common Market Law Review*, 51, 5, pp. 1343–1380.

Scott, J. (2014b) "Extraterritoriality and territorial extension in EU law", *American Journal of Comparative Law*, 62, 1, pp. 87–126.

Shaffer, G. (2000) 'Globalization and social protection: The impact of EU and international rules in the ratcheting up of US data privacy standards,' *Yale Journal of International Law*, 25, pp. 1–88.

Simmons, B. A. (2001) "The international politics of harmonization: The case of capital market regulation," *International Organization*, 55, 3, pp. 589–620.

Spar, D.L. and Bussgang, J. J. (1996) "Ruling the net," *Harvard Business Review*, May/July, pp. 123–133.

Society for Worldwide Interbank Financial Transactions (SWIFT) (2005) "SWIFT Annual Report 2005." Available at www.swift.com/about_swift/publications/annual_reports/annual_report_2005/SWIFT_AR_2005.pdf.

Society for Worldwide Interbank Financial Transactions (SWIFT) (2007a) "SWIFT announces plans for system re-architecture," press release, June 15. Available at www.swift.com/about_swift/legal/compliance/statements_on_compliance/swift_announces_plans_for_system_re_architecture.page?

Society for Worldwide Interbank Financial Transactions (SWIFT) (2007b) "SWIFT completes transparency improvements and obtains registration for Safe Harbor," press release, July 20. Available at www.swift.com/about_swift/legal/compliance/statements_on_compliance/swift_completes_transparency_improvements_and_files_for_safe_harbor/index.page?

Society for Worldwide Interbank Financial Transactions (SWIFT) (2007c) "SWIFT board approves messaging re-architecture," press release, October 4. Available at www.swift.com/about_swift/legal/compliance/statements_on_compliance/swift_board_approves_messaging_re_architecture/index.page?

Society for Worldwide Interbank Financial Transactions (SWIFT) (2008) "SWIFT respects data protection legislation," December 10. Available at www.swift.com/about_swift/press_room/swift_news_archive/home_page_stories_archive_2008/swift_respects_data_protection_legislation.page?

Spanish Presidency (2010) "The EU and the United States sign the agreement on the transfer of bank data (SWIFT)." Available at www.eu2010.es/en/documentosynoticias/noticias/jun28swift.html.

Suda, Y. (2013) "Transatlantic politics of data transfer: Extraterritoriality, counter-extraterritoriality and counter-terrorism," *Journal of Common Market Studies*, 51, 4, pp. 772–788.

Svantesson, D. J. B. (2014) 'The extraterritoriality of EU data privay law: Its theoretical justification and its practical effect on US businesses," *Stanford Journal of International Law*, 50, 1, pp. 53–102.

Swire, P. P. and Litan, R. (1998) *None of Your Business: World Data Flows, Electronic Commerce, and the European Privacy Protection*, Washington, DC: Brookings Institution Press.

United States Customs and Border Protection (CBP) (2008) "CSI fact sheet." Available at www.cbp.gov/xp/cgov/trade/cargo_security/csi.

United States Department of Commerce (2000) "Commerce Secretary William M. Daley hails US–EU "Safe Harbor" privacy arrangement," press release, March 14.

United States Department of Commerce (2016) "Statement from US Secretary of Commerce Penny Pritzker on EU–US Privacy Shield," February 2. Available at www.commerce.gov/news/press-releases/2016/02/statement-us-secretary-commerce-penny-pritzker-eu-us-privacy-shield.

United StatesDepartment of Homeland Security (n.d.) "Frequently Asked Questions regarding Customs and Border Protection receipt of Passenger Name Records related to flights between the European Union and the United States." Available at www.dhs.gov/xlibrary/assets/privacy/privacy_faq_pnr_cbp.pdf.

United States Department of Homeland Security (2003) "Homeland Security and European Commission Reach PNR Agreement." Available at www.dhs.gov/xnews/releases/press_release_0322.shtm.

United States Department of Treasury (n.d.) "Terrorist Finance Tracking Program: Questions and answers." Available at http://useu.usmission.gov/media/pdfs/summary_qa_halfpg_62410.pdf.

United States Securities and Exchange Commission (2012), "Hedge fund manager to pay $44 million for illegal trading in Chinese bank stocks", press release. Available at www.sec.gov/News/PressRelease/Detail/PressRelease/13651714.

Weiss, M. and Archick, K. (2016) "US–EU data privacy: From Safe Harbor to Privacy Shield," Congressional Research Service Report, R44257.

Wesseling, M. (2014) "Evaluation of EU measures to combat terrorist financing in-depth analysis for the LIBE committee." Available at www.europarl.europa.eu/RegData/etudes/note/join/2014/509978/IPOL-LIBE_NT(2014)509978_EN.pdf.

White House (2010) "Remarks by Vice President Biden to the European Parliament," Brussels, May 6. Available at www.whitehouse.gov/the-press-office/remarks-vice-president-biden-european-parliament.

Working Party on the Protection of Individuals with regard to the Processing of Personal Data (1999a) "OPINION 1/99 Concerning the level of data protection in the United States and the ongoing discussions between the European Commission and the United States Government," 5092/98/EN/final WP 15, adopted on January 26.

Working Party on the Protection of Individuals with regard to the Processing of Personal Data (1999b) "Opinion 2/99 on the adequacy of the "International Safe Harbor Principles" issued by the US Department of Commerce on 19th April 1999," 5047/99/EN/final WP 19, adopted on May 3.

Young, A. R. (2015) "Liberalizing trade, not exporting rules: The limits to regulatory co-ordination in the EU's 'new generation' preferential trade agreements," *Journal of European Public Policy*, 22, 9, pp. 1253–1275.

Index

9/11 *see* September 11, 2001, terrorist attacks

Aaron, David 41
accountability principle 14
adequate level of protection: country- and organization-based criteria for 41; determination of 32, 119n1 (*see also* European Commission, adequacy decisions by); EU insistence on 4, 6, 22, 32, 38, 67, 114; and PNRs 57; US as lacking 6, 27, 51–2, 110
air travel: transatlantic 56–7, 86, 112–13; within EU 65, 74–5, 77
Alcoa case 21, 28n4
Amado, Luis 58
anti-corruption laws 22
Antigua and Barbuda 29n13
anti-trust laws 21–2
APEC (Asia-Pacific Economic Cooperation) 101, 108n21
API (Advance Passenger Information) 66, 69n16, 80n2
Argentina 20, 23, 66, 70n20, 119n1
Article 29 Working Party 33–4; on PNR data 58, 60, 62–3, 72; on Privacy Shield 50–1; on Safe Harbor framework 40, 45, 47; and SWIFT 83
assets, and extraterritoriality 23
audit committee independence 29n14
Australia: electronic health records in 117; PNR agreements with 66, 113
authority, transborder claims of 19
Aviation and Transportation Security Act 56

BBBOnline 44
Belgium: data protection law of 92n4; PNR system of 79; Privacy Commission of 83
BEUC (European Consumer Organization) 98
Biden, Joe 88
biometric identification 27
blocking legislation 26
Bolkestein, Fritz 42, 57
border security 4–6, 72
Brazil 66
Bretton, Thierry 119
Bruguière, Jean-Louis 93

Canada: data protection laws of 10; PNR agreements with 66, 78, 113
CBP (Customs and Border Protection) 55–8, 62, 69n12
Chertoff, Michael 58, 62
China: data transfer requirements in 117; and EU ETS 26
civil liberties 16, 18n6, 63–4, 68n1, 69n14, 87
CJEU (Court of Justice of the European Union): on data retention period 80n4; and PNR agreement 7, 58, 60; and Schrems case 46–7, 52, 53n17
cloud computing 1
co-decision procedure 73–4
CoE (Council of Europe) Convention No. 108 12–14, 16
collection limitation principle 13
commercial interests: and data privacy 3–4, 8, 12, 109; and encryption 18n6
Council Framework Decisions 72–3, 77–8, 80n9
Council of the EU 57–8, 65–6, 68n3, 74

counter-extraterritoriality 5–6, 8, 24–5, 115–16
counterterrorism: EU-US agreements on 4–6; extraterritorial reach of 55–6, 115; and personal data 4–5, 15–17; TFTP and PNR agreements and 7–8, 59, 71, 88, 111–12
crime, transnational 19, 59, 63, 75–6, 80n8
CSI (Container Security Initiative) 68n1
Cuba, US sanctions on 26

Daley, William M. 42
databases, active and dormant 59, 61, 72, 77–8
data collection, bulk 50, 52, 75
data havens 12, 30
data integrity principle 43, 48
data localization 97, 102–3, 105, 116–19, 119–20n3
data mining 63, 84, 88
data politics, transatlantic 8
data portability, right of 35
data privacy: EU protections for 31, 33; and FTAs 9, 104; international frameworks for 12–14, 16, 42; as policy problem 10–12, 17; politics of 2–4, 8, 15, 109–10, 116; and public security 3–4, 8, 14–17, 32, 55, 59, 92; transatlantic differences in 38–41, 59, 94, 98; use of term 17n1
Data Privacy and Protection Agreement *see* Umbrella Agreement
data-processing activities 114
data protection: adequate level of *see* adequate level of protection; first-pillar directive on 58; and FTAs 98–100, 104, 106; principles of 13–14, 16, 67, 85, 112; as right 31; transnational 95; use of term 10
data protection authorities: in EU 35, 39–40, 49, 53n12, 60; and PNR issue 58, 60; and Safe Harbor agreement 47; and SWIFT affair 87
data protection laws 10
data protection officers 76–7
Data Protection Package 80n5
data protection policy 67, 96, 113
data quality principle 13, 43, 83
data retention period 58, 66, 73–4, 76–8, 80n4
data subjects: of EU 32, 52; in OECD Guidelines 13
data transfer: bulk 81, 89–90, 116; EU regulations on 32–3, 37, 53n6; future of transatlantic 119; illegal 60; push and pull methods of 62–3, 69nn11,13, 70n22, 76–7, 86–7, 116; transatlantic negotiations on 39–40, 92, 109–10; *see also* free flows of data; transborder flows of data; onward transfer; third-country transfers
Declaration on Combating Terrorism 69n5, 71–2, 84
Department of Commerce (US) 41–2, 44, 47–9, 85
depersonalization 77
derogations 16, 33, 53n6
DHS (Department of Homeland Security): negotiations with European Commission 57; and PNR data 2, 7, 55, 58–9, 61–2, 69n12, 111–12; and SWIFT affair 87
digital trade *see* electronic commerce
dispute resolution mechanisms 46, 48
DOJ (Department of Justice) 23, 48–50
domestic integrity argument 21–2
drug trafficking 19

ECJ (European Court of Justice) *see* CJEU
EDPS (European Data Protection Supervisor): and PNR data 60, 73–5; and SWIFT affair 83; and TTIP 98
EDRi (European Digital Rights) 98
EEA (European Economic Area) 21, 28n4, 85
EFF (Electronic Frontier Foundation) 103
EFTA (European Free Trade Association) 118
e-government 11
electronic commerce: barriers to 94–6; market power in 24; and personal data 7, 11–12, 45, 55, 114; and Safe Harbor 51; in TiSA 105; under TPP 102–3, 108n24; US stance on 40, 96–7
EMIR (European Market Instrument Regulation) 22
encryption 15, 18n6
espionage, industrial and economic 84, 93n10
EU (European Union): biometric passports in 27; Charter of Fundamental Rights 37n3; creation of Single Market 30–1; data

principles 6, 41, 59–60, 67; data protection rules of 2–4, 30–1, 34–5, 39, 96, 115–16 (*see also* EU Data Protection Directive; General Data Protection Regulation); ETS (Emissions Trading System) 21–3, 26; extraterritorial influence of 5, 22–4, 52, 113–14; FTAs and data privacy 101; pillars of 58, 60, 68–9n4; *see also* European Commission
EU Data Protection Directive 8; adequacy decisions under *see* European Commission, adequacy decisions by; Belgian implementation of 92n4; extraterritoriality of 22, 25, 32–3, 38–40, 51–2, 68, 110; formulation of 30–1, 37n6; influence of 36; national privacy protectors under 33–4; and PNRs 56–7, 59; and regulatory capacity 24; replacement for *see* General Data Protection Regulation; rules under 31–2, 53n4, 95, 118; and Safe Harbor agreement 2, 5–7, 27, 43; and SWIFT affair 83, 112
EU Data Retention Directive 15, 80n4
EU PNR Directive 9, 64–5, 75–80, 80n7
European Commission: adequacy decisions by 32–6, 41–2, 50–1, 58; and FTA negotiations 98–100, 104; and PNR data 60, 63–5, 68n2, 71–3, 78, 80n12; regulation of mergers 21; and Safe Harbor framework 39–43, 45–7; and terrorist financing 84–6, 90–1, 93n6; and transparency 48
European Convention on Human Rights 37n2, 39, 56, 74
European Council 80n1; and data sharing with US 69n14; and PNR data 69n5, 72–3, 75; and SWIFT affair 87–8; on terrorist financing 84
European Parliament: on data sharing for law enforcement 69n14; and FTA negotiations 99, 104; and NSA scandal 64, 91; and PNR data 7, 58, 60–1, 63–4, 70n21, 73–7; and SWIFT affair 83–4, 86–8, 93n9; and TFTP 8, 90; on transatlantic data flows 45–6, 51, 53n15; and Umbrella Agreement 66
European Terrorist Finance Tracking System 89–90
Europe-only cloud 118–19
Europol 76, 89
externalities, negative 21
extraterritoriality: based on nationality 20; effectiveness of 27–8; effects-based 21–2; of EU data protection rules 36, 118; logic of 8, 19, 25; of US counterterrorism 111
extraterritorial regulation: distributional impact of 28; politics of 3–6, 8, 19, 109–10; responses to 25–7; sources of 22–4; of transactional conduct 20

FCPA (Foreign Corrupt Practices Act) 20, 22, 28n9
financial services 12, 95, 97, 104–5, 114
financial transaction data: EU-US negotiations on 4, 9, 87, 91–2; intra-European 86; and personal information 7; SWIFT storage of 82
FOIA (Freedom of Information Act) 61, 69n8
foreign fighters 75, 79
Framework for Global Electronic Commerce 40
France 10, 21, 26
Frattini, Franco 85
free flows of data 31, 94–5, 103, 106, 117; *see also* transborder flows of data
FTAs (free trade agreements), and data privacy 9, 94–5, 101–2, 105–6, 114
FTC (Federal Trade Commission) 44, 48–9, 54n20

GATS (General Agreement on Trade in Services) 100, 104
General Data Protection Regulation 8, 30, 34–7, 95, 114, 118–19
Germany, data protection laws in 10

Hague Program 71
Holder, Eric 63–4

IEEPA (International Emergency Economic Powers Act) 82, 92n2
individual participation principle 14
industry self-regulation 27, 39–41, 44, 51, 111
information-based economy 7, 55
information exchange 30, 57, 65, 68
information gathering 15–16, 52, 81
insider trading 21–2
intellectual property 19, 94–6, 101, 107n7

internet: penetration of 1; regionalization of 119
"Internetz" 118
interoperability 98, 105
Iran, US sanctions on 26

Japan: and anti-corruption regulation 20, 25; data protection laws of 10; PNR agreements with 66; and TPP 103
Jourová, Věra 47
Judicial Redress Act 66

law enforcement: and data localization 117; personal data used for 4, 8, 11, 15, 80n2, 92; and PNR data 63, 67–8, 71–3, 75, 79; and Privacy Shield 49
law enforcement authorities, information sharing between 1, 69n14
letter exchange format 84
LIBE Committee 74–5
Libya, US sanctions on 26
Lisbon Treaty 37, 60, 73, 88, 91, 93n7
localization barriers to trade 96–7, 107n7, 118
London, bombings of 2005 71, 79

Madrid, bombings of 2004 69n5, 71, 79
market power 22–4, 28
meals, choice of 55, 69n6
Mexico, PNR agreements with 66
mirror servers 82, 85
money laundering 19, 23, 28n7

national security: and data localization 117; and encryption 15; in EU Data Protection Directive 32; in OECD Guidelines 16; and Privacy Shield 49
necessity and proportionality 72–4, 80
NFTC (National Foreign Trade Council) 97
non-tariff barriers to trade 94–6, 101
NSA (National Security Agency), mass surveillance scandal 7–8, 45, 64, 91, 97–8

Obama, Barack 50, 66, 103, 106nn3-4
ODA (official development assistance) 20
ODNI (Office of the Director of National Intelligence) 48–51
OECD (Organization for Economic Co-operation and Development): establishment of 17n2; Privacy Guidelines 12–14, 16, 17–18nn5,9, 43, 53n11
OFAC (Office of Foreign Assets Control) 81
onward transfers: of PNR data 63; in Privacy Shield Principles 48; in Safe Harbor Principles 42, 45
OPA (Online Privacy Alliance) 44, 53n13
openness principle 13–14

Paris, terrorist attacks of 2015 in 65, 75–6, 79
PATRIOT Act 15, 18n7, 28n7
personal data: EU regulations on 31–2, 34–5, 37n4, 52, 112; and FTAs 95, 100, 102; international conventions on 12–14, 47–8, 66–7; law enforcement use of 15–17; limits on processing and use 10–11, 110, 114–15, 117; public and private use of 8; transatlantic negotiations on 2–4, 38, 40–1, 55, 92; transborder flows of 1–2, 11–12; transfer to third countries *see* onward transfers; third-country transfers; *see also* sensitive data
personal information *see* personal data
PIUs (Passenger Information Units) 72–7
PNR (Passenger Name Records): in EU member states 79, 80 n12; EU policy on 9, 71–5, 80n5 (*see also* EU PNR Directive); and extraterritoriality 6, 20, 111; global agreements on 66–7, 113; and territoriality 115–16; transatlantic accords on 2, 4–5, 7–8, 55, 57–62, 65, 67–8, 77–8, 109, 112–13; transmission of 62–3; US requests for 55–6, 68n1
pornography, child 19
PPD-28 50
PRISM program 45, 64, 91
Pritzker, Penny 47
privacy, forms of 17n1; *see also* data privacy
Privacy Act (US) 10, 39, 66, 69n8
privacy-invasive practices 12
privacy laws, international differences between 1–2
privacy policies, of companies 46, 52n2
privacy rights: and encryption 15; in Europe 31; and personal data 10–11; transatlantic differences in 39

Privacy Shield: adequacy decision on 50–1; and Safe Harbor 4, 7–8, 38, 47–8, 52; US benefits from 111
Privacy Shield List 49
Privacy Shield Ombudsperson 49
Privacy Shield Principles 48–9
profiling 35, 63, 84
proportionality principle: and PNRs 58–9, 75, 79; and SWIFT affair 87, 116; *see also* necessity and proportionality
protectors of privacy 33–4, 58; *see also* data protection officers
public security: and adequate level of protection 35; and data privacy 3–4, 8, 14–17, 32, 55, 59, 92; in EU Data Protection Directive 32; and PNRs 56, 58
purpose limitation principle 48, 56, 63, 66–7
purpose specification principle 13

Al-Qa'ida 86

reciprocity deficit 64–5
Reding, Viviane 98
redress mechanisms: and TFTP 86; under Privacy Shield 49; under Safe Harbor 46
regulation, convergence in 28n5
regulatory capacity 24, 28n11
rights to regulate 103, 106
right to be forgotten 35, 37n10
risk assessment 55
RTAs (regional trade agreements) 94
Russia: personal data law in 117; PNR agreements with 66

Safe Harbor framework: adequacy decisions under 41; choice under 53n11; consumer groups and 53n14; creation of 6–8, 38, 42, 51–2, 110–11; and data privacy 4, 109; enforcement of 43–4; and extraterritoriality 5–6, 27; and SWIFT 85
Safe Harbor Principles 6, 41–6, 48
SAFE Port Act 20, 22
Sarbanes-Oxley Act 25, 27, 29nn12,14
Saudi Arabia, PNR agreements with 66
Schengen Area, virtual 118–19, 120nn4–5
Schrems, Maximillian 46–7
SEC (Securities and Exchange Commission) 23
security cooperation, trans-Atlantic 6
security safeguards principle 13
sensitive data: in EU Data Protection Rules 31, 59; in EU PNR directive 76; in PNR accords 61, 69nn6,7, 78; in Privacy Shield Principles 48; in Safe Harbor Arrangement 42; use of term 53n9
sensitive information *see* sensitive data
SEPA (Single European Payment Area) 87, 89
September 11, 2001, terrorist attacks 2, 7–8, 15, 55, 81, 111
Sherman Antitrust Act 28n4
Snowden, Edward 44–6, 118
social regulation, philosophies of 39
South Korea: data protection laws of 10, 117; FTA with EU 101, 106, 114; PNR agreements with 66
state sovereignty 115
Stockholm Program 73
supranational institutions 29n13
surveillance: NSA program of 45; and personal data 15
Sweden 10
SWIFT (Society for Worldwide Interbank Financial Transactions): and extraterritoriality 6, 111; headquarters of 92; NSA access to 91; redesign of network 85–6; and territoriality 115–16; and TFTP 2, 4–5, 7–9, 81–4; transatlantic talks over 84–8, 109, 112–13; use of data from 92
Switzerland 85, 108n28, 119n1, 120n

TACD (Transatlantic Consumer Dialogue) 53n14
territoriality: and data privacy 119–20n3; and globalization 21, 115–16; sovereign principle of 19, 24; *see also* extraterritoriality
terrorism, transnational 15–16; *see also* counterterrorism
terrorist financing 4–5, 81, 83–4, 92; *see also* TFTP
TFEU (Treaty on the Functioning of the European Union) 37n4
TFTP (Terrorist Finance Tracking Program): Bruguière on 93n6; and data transfer 116; EU-US agreements on 2, 4–5, 7–9, 85–92, 109; resistance to 63, 82–4; and SWIFT data 81–2, 111–12

third-country transfers: and data localization 117; and EU Data Protection Directive 32–3, 38–40, 53n4, 57, 110, 118; EU requirements for 63, 80n9, 84; and General Data Protection Regulation 35–6, 114–15; and PNR agreement 76; and TTIP 98
TiSA (Trade in Services Agreement) 94, 104–6, 108n28
TPA (Trade Promotion Authority) 96, 107n5
TPP (Trans-Pacific Partnership): and data localization 103, 117; data protection and privacy in 9, 94, 102–3; fast-track authority for 96; fate of 103; negotiations on 101–2, 106, 108n20
transatlantic trade, and data transfer 40
transborder flows, regulation of 19
transborder flows of data: conflicts between jurisdictions on 17, 17–18n5; and EU regulations 36, 118; and FTAs 94–9, 102–6, 106n4, 108n25; and localization 116; privacy guidelines on 12–14; transatlantic 39–40, 44–7, 51, 53n3, 65, 110; *see also* free flows of data; personal data
transnational corporations 1, 12
transparency 46, 48, 67
Treasury Department (US): and North Korea sanctions 28n7; and SWIFT affair 2, 7, 81–6, 88–9, 111–13, 115
Trump, Donald 100, 103
TRUSTe 44
TTIP (Transatlantic Trade and Investment Partnership): data protection and privacy in 9, 94, 106; negotiations on 95–6, 98–101, 106n3, 107–8n19

UK (United Kingdom): data privacy in 10; and extraterritoriality 21; PNR system of 78–9
Umbrella Agreement 65–6, 69n15, 110
United Arab Emirates 66
United States: counterterrorism efforts 5, 7–9, 67, 111–13, 115; data rules of 2–6, 10, 27, 39, 110–11; and extraterritoriality 5, 21–2, 26–7; finance sector of 23–4; in FTA negotiations 96–8, 103–6, 107n5; hegemonic behaviors by 6; intelligence agencies of 45–6, 49–50, 52, 91, 117–18 (*see also* NSA; ODNI); investment in EU 52n3; mass surveillance programs of 100; privacy regime of 5, 40, 51; and transborder data flows 17–18n5; Visa Waiver Program 61; *see also* Department of Commerce; DHS; DOJ; Treasury Department
UNPA (United Nations Participation Act) 82, 92n3
use limitation principle 13, 43
USTR (United States Trade Representative) 96, 103–4

values, fundamental 11–12
Vietnam, data localization in 117

Working Party on the Protection of Individuals with regard to the Processing of Personal Data *see* Article 29 Working Party
WTO (World Trade Organization): and data privacy 100; and Internet gambling 29n13; and RTAs 94–5; and TiSA 104, 108n30

For Product Safety Concerns and Information please contact our EU representative GPSR@taylorandfrancis.com
Taylor & Francis Verlag GmbH, Kaufingerstraße 24, 80331 München, Germany

www.ingramcontent.com/pod-product-compliance
Lightning Source LLC
LaVergne TN
LVHW020629300926
849161LV00004B/652

* 9 7 8 1 1 3 8 6 9 6 2 8 0 *